MONEY
TALKS

MONEY

JULIETTE FAIRLEY

BLACK FINANCE EXPERTS TALK TO YOU ABOUT MONEY

TALKS

John Wiley & Sons, Inc.

New York • Chichester • Weinheim • Brisbane • Singapore • Toronto

Copyright © 1998 by Juliette Fairley. All rights reserved.
Published by John Wiley & Sons, Inc.

Published simultaneously in Canada.

This publication is designed to provide accurate and authoritative information in regard to the subject matter covered. It is sold with the understanding that the publisher is not engaged in rendering legal, accounting, or other professional services. If legal advice or other expert assistance is required, the services of a competent professional person should be sought.

Library of Congress Cataloging-in-Publication Data:

Fairley, Juliette, 1966–
    Money talks : black finance experts talk to you about
money / Juliette Fairley.
      p. cm.
    Includes index.
    ISBN 0-471-24582-8 (cloth : alk. paper)
    1. Afro-Americans—Finance, Personal. 2. Finance, Personal.
I. Title.
HG179.F328 1998
332.024'0396073—dc21   97-45917

Printed in the United States of America

10 9 8 7 6 5 4 3 2 1

To
MY PARENTS
and
TO CHILDREN
who have no idea
what awaits them financially
in adulthood

Contents

Part IV GOVERNMENT

Part V MONEY/INVESTMENT MANAGEMENT

Part VI TRADING

foreword

I F WE BLACKS LOOK AT OUR STRUGGLE FOR FREEDOM as a musical composition, the first movement was marked by the end of slavery. The second focused on civil rights. The third stage was the fight for the right to vote. We are in the fourth movement of our composition today—the struggle for economic inclusion, opportunity, and fairness.

The Rainbow/Push Coalition launched the Wall Street Project to move America past its long history of denying blacks and people of color access to the marketplace. Though not often discussed, Wall Street was deeply involved in the slave trade. About 60 New York clothing firms were doing business in the South as late as 1860, on the eve of the Civil War. Several New York firms were branches of Southern firms, and many New York businessmen and firms owned slaves and plantations in the South. The *New York Journal of Commerce* commented on February 19, 1860, that New York was "almost as dependent upon Southern slavery as Charleston itself."

Many New York merchants were extensively interested in the slave trade between Cuba and the coast of Africa. Business firms of the highest repute supplied capital for these ventures. In fact, the first investment bankers raised money for slave ships. When slavery was abolished, many of those companies began to trade the products of slaves, as cotton brokers.

So, Wall Street helped to create the problem our government is still trying to resolve. Wall Street took part in America's original sin—slavery. And although the laws changed, patterns of exclusion did not. The patterns of restraint of trade did not change.

That's why the Rainbow/Push Coalition's economic office is on Wall Street. We are building a permanent presence with a professional staff and allies. The issue is not just race and sex discrimination; it is restraint of trade. When trade is restrained, growth is limited. Discrimination and lack of free trade because of racial barriers cost the American economy at least $60 billion every year.

Through a process of research, education, coordination, and negotiation, we're monitoring the hiring, promotion, and purchasing practices of Fortune 1000 companies. We are not looking for charity, but rather parity. We target companies for fairness and for reciprocal trade relationships. We are not looking for boycott targets, but when companies boycott us we must reciprocate as a way of opening up the marketplace.

America did not hesitate to use economic leverage on Japan; the world community did not hesitate to use economic leverage on South Africa. Dr. Martin Luther King used economic leverage on Montgomery, Alabama, and Rainbow/Push used it on Texaco and Mitsubishi. We intend, like Joshua, to march around the walls, seven days and seven nights, until the walls come tumbling down.

As the walls come down, we must be vigilant about

making the money we earn work for us. We need the capacity to pass our successes on to succeeding generations. So many wealthy whites inherited their fortunes. A whole body of law deals with inheritance taxes. We blacks don't have many pages in that book.

Reading *Money Talks* could well be a major step toward building your net worth and keeping the wealth in the family! Here's to an interesting and profitable read. Keep hope alive!

REV. JESSE L. JACKSON, SR.
Founder and President
Rainbow/Push Coalition
September 16, 1997

Acknowledgments

THIS BOOK WOULDN'T HAVE BEEN POSSIBLE WITHOUT the input of all the finance experts featured in the book, and many thanks to Jesse Jackson, Sr., for the Foreword. A shout-out to Derek Dingle who led me to Debby Englander. Thank you, Debby, for taking a chance on an unknown author. Many thanks to Marie Brown, who negotiated the contract and led me through the labyrinth of my first book deal.

During the course of the seven months spent writing and interviewing, I had moral support from several people. They include my parents and my sister Dorothy.

Some other people who were real gems throughout this process include Joya Whitehead, the Gaylors, Lise Funderberg, Dr. Grace Cornish, Tony Chappelle, Mike Smart, Leroy Thompson, Harry Davis, and Chee Chee Williams.

Introduction

MONEY TALKS IS A BOOK THAT I HAVE BEEN THINK-ing about writing for some time. I've spent nearly a decade reporting and writing about personal finance. Along the way, I have been fortunate to interview some of the leading planners, bankers, financiers, and other experts in the business world. I've taken some of their advice and hopefully have put it to good use in my personal life.

What I hope this book does is give people a practical notion of how to save more of their money and invest it with greater care. To help readers expand their financial wisdom, I've turned to prominent African-American business experts and asked for their advice.

Although much of the finance advice in this book is applicable to a wide range of readers, I especially wanted to address African-American readers. According to an independent poll conducted by Roper Starch Worldwide, African-Americans are more risk-averse than non African-Americans when it comes to investing. Furthermore, this study shows that only 22% of blacks invest in mutual funds compared to 35% of whites, and only 27% of blacks invest in stocks and bonds compared to 38% of whites.

While I can't fully explain the reasons for these statistics, I feel that by interviewing a range of prominent, successful, and in some cases exceedingly wealthy black professionals, I might help black readers to be inspired and motivated to make changes in the way they handle their personal finances.

In selecting people to interview for *Money Talks*, I looked for a range of individuals who worked in different arenas, followed varied investment strategies, and had interesting career paths. The common thread among all these experts: their success, whether it is measured in dollar terms—John Rogers, CEO of Ariel Capital, whose net worth is more than $10 million, and Harold Doley, chairman of Doley Securities, whose estimated net worth is $25 million—or accomplishments—Maceo Sloan, who started the first African-American–owned money management firm in North Carolina, and Dr. Emma Chappell, the first African-American woman to start a full-service commercial bank.

There are also profiles of people who faced problems more familiar to many readers. For example, Glinda Bridgforth runs a multimillion-dollar consulting company serving as financial planner, and she has a mini-empire revolving around her motivational and personal growth seminars, tapes, and publications. But Bridgforth herself only began her career after going through a divorce and weathering a financial crisis.

While I had a set of questions to ask each interviewee, I found that people often strayed from a particular query in order to emphasize certain points. Still, there were key issues that I wanted people to address: I wanted these experts to offer their best financial advice for African-Americans—whether it be savings strategies or tips on investing. I also wanted the interviewees to talk about their personal finances. Some people were very forthcoming and openly discussed their investment styles, portfolio holdings, and net worth. Others preferred not to disclose their personal money habits.

To help you make the most of the sage counsel from these prominent individuals, I use several editorial devices to make this information accessible. Each chapter ends with "The Last Word," which is the expert's response to my query about the most important financial step for African-Americans to take. In addition, when there is specific personal finance information such as explanations of financial strategies or tax issues, I have boxed these facts. The experts' own financials are included in "Personal Portfolio" sections while their specific advice is in "Financial Advice" and "Investing Advice" sections. The profiles are grouped by profession—accounting, banking, financial planning, government, money management, and trading stocks and bonds.

Money Talks is an important and empowering tool. African-Americans must join the revolution by educating themselves about investing. The power is in the money, and the more money you have, the more opportunities you will have, regardless of what you endeavor to achieve. My hope is that this book will motivate you to join the next frontier of the civil rights movement—economic inclusion—by taking charge of your finances.

JULIETTE FAIRLEY
September 15, 1997

Part I

ACCOUNTING

Chapter 1

Bert Mitchell is the founder, chairman, and CEO of Mitchell & Titus, LLP, CPAs, and management consultants. He received his B.B.A. and M.B.A. from the City University of New York. He currently resides in Oyster Bay, New York, with his wife and three children.

BERT MITCHELL

ERT MITCHELL IS THE FOUNDER, CHAIRMAN, AND chief executive officer of Mitchell & Titus, LLP, the nation's largest minority-owned accounting firm. The firm also ranks among the 40 largest certified public accountant (CPA) firms in the United States and has a staff of more than 200 in New York City, Washington, DC, and Philadelphia.

Mitchell's clients include entertainer Michael Jackson, the Dance Theater of Harlem, the National Urban League, the Free Library of Philadelphia, Black Enterprise, PepsiCo, Bristol-Myers, CBS, Kodak, and Innercity Broadcasting.

A native of Jamaica, West Indies, Mitchell migrated to the United States in 1958. He earned bachelor's and master's degrees from the Bernard M. Baruch College of the City University of New York. He is also a graduate of the Owner-President Management Program of the Harvard Business School.

He started his firm in 1973 after serving as a partner in the oldest black CPA firm until 1972. Mitchell borrowed $65,000 from a Minority Enterprise Small Business Investment Company (MESBIC), which was a creation of the Nixon administration in the 1970s to help blacks start their own businesses.

"Most investments that MESBICs made failed, but we were successful. We were able to pay back our debt. They didn't lose any money on us. Eight out of every ten cases were a loss. We were fortunate that MESBICs were around. We started developing a clientele and tried to hire the best people we could find. As a firm, we were disposed to dispersing ownership of the firm and over the years, we took additional partners, which is significant among black-owned business because most successful black-owned businesses are family businesses," he says. "We built our clientele because I had a reputation as a CPA. I was active in the profession and had done a lot of writing. I was pretty good at what I do."

PERSONAL PORTFOLIO

Mitchell's most important investment is his business. Aside from that, he has also invested in stocks, mutual funds, municipal bonds, and real estate. He says that real estate is generally a good investment as long as you don't have to sell at any particular time. Some of the stock he owns include General Electric, International Paper, Intel, and Compaq. "I buy stocks on a long-term basis. I don't buy them to sell them six months later. I buy good companies that I'm going to keep for a long time," he says.

Mitchell is chairman of the board of the Ariel Mutual Fund Family (see Chapter 15, on John Rogers). In addition to being invested in Ariel mutual funds, he's also invested in T. Rowe Price and Fidelity funds. "I buy stocks, like General Electric, that are perceived to be well managed companies that are always going to perform over the long haul. I look for a company that has historically good management and reasonable price-to-earnings ratio," he says. "In terms of technology stocks, look for companies that are on the cutting edge, where market psychology will continue to make the stock go up. Basically stocks go up because of increased earnings or because of market psychology because people think they are going to go up. With market psychology, people make stocks go up because people are willing to pay more for them. With technology stocks, there's a lot of market psychology. You have stocks that have never earned a dime that are selling for a bunch of money."

Mitchell says that his largest holding and favorite stock is Compaq because they have a good product and are innovative. "A lot of times you can make investments in stocks by looking at products around you. I had a marketing professor at Harvard who used to say 'walk Third Avenue' to look at the stores and see what people are buying. If you have a product that you like, buy stock in it. I like Intel because they are a critical part of the technology business in terms of making the chips," he says. "You can earn 10 to 12 percent in the market by buying stock and holding it. Most of the money is made in the stock market by people who don't sell."

Examples of some of the stocks that Mitchell is still reaping benefits from are MCI, Philip Morris, and Telemex, a Mexican telephone company. Mitchell bought MCI 10 years ago for $5 per share. Today, it's worth $35. He bought Philip Morris 10 years ago for $10 and now it's worth $45. Telemex, Mitchell bought for $4 a share 12 years ago and now it's worth $50.

Mitchell scoffs at a savings account. He says he doesn't have one. Instead, he puts the money he doesn't want to spend into investments. In terms of unconventional investments, such as artwork, Mitchell says he buys artwork for enjoyment. "I'm an art collector. I happen to have a very sizable investment in artwork but I don't buy art for investment. I buy art because I like it. I suspect that most of the art I have is worth more than what I bought it for. I buy art because I want to look at it," he says.

Mitchell says African-Americans need to consider charitable contributions to nonprofit organizations that are trying to improve the lot of everyone. "I give a substantial amount of dollars, like in the tens of thousands, to charity on an annual basis. Black people do give mostly to the church but we need to give outside of the church as well. Consider the NAACP, the National Urban League, and schools. I give money to my elementary school in the Caribbean. Giving is a big part of the gratification of success and it seems that the more you give, the more you have," he says.

INVESTING ADVICE: THE POWER OF OWNERSHIP

Mitchell also thinks that ownership is an important theme for African-Americans going into the 21st century. In fact, with a $50,000 inheritance, Mitchell recommends trying to get into an ownership situation by buying a home or starting a business. "If you think you understand what that business might be about, but I wouldn't go into a frivolous business with it," he warns.

In terms of pitfalls, Mitchell says people don't leverage what they own because they are risk-averse. As a result, opportunities just pass them by. "For example, if you have a house that has no mortgage and that's fully paid up, you can take some of your equity out of that and invest in something else and let it grow for you at the same time. You should try, within reason, to leverage your capital. You could take a loan against your house to start your business, or invest in some other real estate or land that has another chance of appreciating," he says.

The problem with leveraging is that it involves some risk. Mitchell says that most black people are risk-averse so they don't leverage. "Black people don't like to owe money. But you give up some opportunities when you are risk-averse," he says.

THE LAST WORD

THE MOST IMPORTANT THING FOR AFRICAN-AMERicans is to get into systematic investing by way of mutual funds and IRAs, Mitchell says.

"They need to put away whatever they can for as long as they possibly can. When your kids graduate from college or high school, open up a mutual fund for them and leave the money there. If you have grandchildren, do the same thing. Just let the money grow," he says.

Another tip Mitchell shares is to open an individual retirement account (IRA) for your child. "If kids start putting money in an IRA when they are 10 years old, 12 years old, or 15 years old, the dollars that they put in there are worth tens of thousands when they are 70 years old. The money just accumulates tax-free," he says. "The key thing is systematic investing. I mention IRAs because it's a tax-deferred investment that accumulates faster than one can ever imagine. I set up an IRA for my son and when he graduated from college, he had $40,000 in it. When he's 70 years old, that IRA will have $6 million in it and he won't have to put one more dime in it."

Part II

BANKING/
CREDIT UNIONS

Chapter 2

Emma Chappell is founder, chairman, president, and CEO of United Bank of Philadelphia. She holds a B.A. from the Berean Institute at Temple University, M.A. from Stonier Graduate School of Banking, D.C.L. from Beaver College, L.L.D. from Lincoln University, H.L.D. from Eastern College, and doctor of humanities from Albright College. She currently resides in Philadelphia, Pennsylvania.

COURTESY OF EMMA CHAPPELL, © BACHRACH

EMMA CHAPPELL

D R. EMMA CHAPPELL IS THE FIRST AFRICAN-AMERI-can woman in America to start a full-service commercial bank. She founded the United Bank of Philadelphia in March of 1992 and serves as chairman, president, and CEO of the bank, which has $101 million in assets.

The motivation to start the bank came from her experience as treasurer of Jesse Jackson's presidential campaign in 1984. She found that every viable African-American community in the United States had a thriving minority-owned financial institution. As part of her push to establish a black bank in Philadelphia, which is 43% black, Chappell conducted a study in 1987. She found that there was $382 million being loaned for mortgages in the city but less than $8 million was going to the African-American community and less than $2 million was going to women in general. "The results of the study indicated that there was tremendous discrimination in Philadelphia as it related to mortgages and small business lending," she says. "There was a need for a black bank."

Chappell started in banking in 1959 right out of high school at the former Continental Bank as a clerk-photographer, photostatting checks, making $45 a week. She worked her way up to vice president in charge of the community business loan and development department, which she established in 1971.

"I saw the influence the bank president had and I said one day I will be president of a bank. I had no idea that I'd start a bank myself, but I had hoped that I would be able to grow up and be in a position to be appointed president of a bank. Starting the bank was difficult. So many people believed it couldn't happen. I had to convince my own community, because there had been about four or five failed attempts to start a bank in years past and people had become apathetic and nonbelievers. When people supported me, it was kind of a last-ditch effort. They said, 'If she doesn't do it, it's probably not going to happen.' The difference was that I had been active in the community in nonprofit organizations and had experience in banking," she says.

Chappell was chairperson of Jesse Jackson's Operation Push board and founding vice president of the National Rainbow Coalition. She helped start the Philadelphia chapter of Operation Push in 1974. "There had been a lot of redlining at the time, and people were disturbed by the neglect that the other banks practiced in the African-American community," she says. "I learned a lot about the community and our people, more than I knew just living in the community. I learned about how we are discriminated against and how we discriminate, and we do discriminate among ourselves, unfortunately."

To start United Bank, Chappell raised the capital by selling stock to the community at $10 a share. She went to churches and community organizations and people's homes to persuade them that Philadelphia needed a financial institution owned and controlled by African-Americans. "I set out to raise $3 million and we ultimately raised $6 million by not only going to the African-American community but getting some of the other banks and insurance companies to buy some preferred stock," she says. The minimum amount to invest in the bank at the time was $500. The average investment was between $500 to $1,000, and the money collected was put into an escrow account in case the bank failed.

"I was working from home. I developed my business plan in my dining room. I met with a lawyer who helped me prepare my offering circular, and we did a private placement to sell the stock," she says. "I had been fortunate to go to graduate school and during that experience, which was right before I became national treasurer to Jesse Jackson, I learned how to operate a bank." Chappell earned a master's degree from the Stonier Graduate School of Banking at Rutgers University. Her thesis, "A Banking Strategy for Minority Business Development," was incorporated into United Bank's business plan.

United Bank stock is not public, and for now Chappell plans to keep it that way. "We currently have three thousand shareholders and that's as public as we want to be for the moment. Being private gives us an opportunity to grow the bank and position ourselves so that we can pay a decent return on the current shareholders' investment," she says. The policy of the bank is to be 75% loan-to-deposit. In actuality, the bank hovers between 72% and 78% loan-to-deposit, which means that if the bank takes in $100 million in deposits, the bank will have $72 to $78 million out in loans. "We currently have $69 million out in loans and most are in mortgages," she says. "We just received an outstanding Community Reinvestment Act (CRA) rating because of that. They say that very often minority banks don't lend to minorities. We were able to prove that we do."

FINANCIAL ADVICE: START SMALL AND KEEP ADDING TO YOUR SAVINGS

Chappell says that what African-Americans need to know is that you can become wealthy by growing your wealth. "You don't have to be born wealthy, but it's like anything else—you have to work at it and you have to plan it. You need to begin early in your life to save, even if it's just $10 a week or $40 a month. Pay yourself first and don't touch it as you accumulate it. Then seek out financial advice from a professional. But, it takes time to do that," she says. "The way you save is to set aside a certain amount of money. Make up your mind to take it off the top when you get paid. See to it that the bank automatically transfers a certain amount out of your checking into your savings account and make that an account that's not going to be touched. You keep building it and then ultimately you put it in some sort of instrument that pays you higher than a bank interest rate. When you get $50,000 or more, seek out someone, a financial adviser, to begin to plan your wealth. All too often African-Americans take money for granted as though it's always going to be there or it's never going to be there. I didn't know how I was going to start the bank, but I sat down and drew out a plan. Everyone should look at their life and develop a plan for the future."

One thing that Chappell has noticed is that people who have money know what they are spending on a daily, weekly, and monthly basis. "They watch what they're spending and they may even keep records of it so that it is controlled. It's like anything else—you have to have a plan. I suggest keeping track of what you spend on a day-to-day basis on food, cosmetics, clothes, and your cleaning bill. At the end of the month, total it up and see if you can save money in given areas. People who don't have money do a lot of impulse spending," she says. "I never have any money on me because my money is planned."

Chappell says the investment that she's still reaping benefits from is her investment in her education. "In the early stages of my life I put aside money for my education using the same method that I'm advising. I put aside money and kept it in a savings account and accumulated it to the point that when I graduated from high school and started my first job, I could then afford to pay for an education at night. It was a great investment. If I hadn't done that, I don't know where I'd be without an education," she says. "I saved consistently and I think that's the key."

PERSONAL PORTFOLIO

Chappell says she's very diversified in mutual funds, stocks, and bonds. She's also heavily invested in the bank. "When we started our bank, I felt that I should show my belief by buying stock myself. I encouraged nine other people to do the same thing. Ten of us put in $50,000 each so that we would have $500,000 in risk capital, whether the bank opened or not; that was money that we could risk," she says.

Chappell was reluctant to discuss her personal finances, insisting that she hasn't amassed a large personal fortune. But, according to *Securities Pro Newsletter*, Chappell is worth more than $5 million. She chose to emphasize the fact that she tries to invest wisely. "I think about what I'm doing. I'm a planner and very analytical and I use those techniques to grow wealth. I'm comfortable, not wealthy," she says. "By analytical, I mean research companies because there may be practices that those companies have that you would not like to invest in even though they might be good investments. They may not be furthering the cause of your people. And that's why I think it's so exciting what Reverend Jackson is doing on Wall Street, encouraging these big companies to consider doing business with the African-American community. The question to ask before investing in a company is, 'Do they do business with us?,' which is critical if we're going to be doing business with them."

In describing her investment technique, Chappell stresses seeking professional advice, using common sense and reading about various companies and their practices before investing. "Find out what's going on in the stock market, and get an overall sense of what's happening in the economy. I always recommend that people save with the intent of investing. We created this bank because we want African-Americans to get back to the basics, and that is to begin to save again, because all Americans have gotten away from the idea of saving. We tend to make our money and then we spend it immediately by buying what we don't need. African-Americans are definitely consumers. We tend to be more consumer-oriented than any other race of people. We need to get away from that and begin to save, invest, and grow our wealth. It's doable. So often, I hear people say, 'But I only make $30,000 a year.' Keep in mind that in 1960, I made $45 a week and still was able to put money away," she says.

Currently, she puts more into investments over savings because she's trying to get ready for retirement. About $50 a week goes into her savings account and $1,000 a month into investments. "Before, I was preparing for education and building wealth for living purposes, and now I'm preparing for retirement. I want to make sure I live well in retirement, so I believe in retirement programs and insurance to make sure that if you get sick, you have some way of being taken care of," she says.

In particular, Chappell says older single people should consider establishing a Standby Trust so as not to be a burden to their children. "I have a trust where money goes into a benefit plan, and the trust, or the bank, determines how my assets are dispersed if I get sick and can't care for myself. It's a phantom trust. It doesn't come into play if I don't get sick, but you never know," she says. "Financial institutions can make decisions over my money, but it's a cotrust with my daughters agreeing."

INVESTING ADVICE

If you have a $50,000 inheritance, Chappell recommends investing it right away in mutual funds. With only $50 a month to invest, she recommends saving it until it reaches the $1,000 mark. After that, proceed to buy a certificate of deposit (CD) or stocks with the help of an investment adviser. "It depends on whether they can put that thousand dollars away for a long term or short term. I recommend savings in banks for short term and investments for longer term," she says.

When selecting a bank, Chappell says it's important to choose one that is Federal Deposit Insurance Corporation (FDIC)-insured. Banks insure up to $100,000. She also says to look for the highest interest rate you can get. "I definitely recommend using black financial institutions, and I don't think we do enough of it. The way we control our financial futures is by putting our money in black-owned financial institutions. These institutions accumulate money and reinvest it back into the community," she says. "We're the ones who ultimately benefit from this collective investment. The greatest advantage to United Bank is you're known and you're not just a number, you're an individual. We know who you are, and when you need a bank to be there for you, United Bank will be there for you because they know you."

Despite changes wrought by the Community Reinvestment Act, Chappell says majority-owned banks can discriminate by pricing their deposit products in a way that excludes African-Americans. "There may be minimum account balances that are too high for African-Americans, and there may be higher interest rates on larger account balances," Chappell says. "Read the fine print."

To sidestep these discriminatory practices, look for banks that offer competitive rates on small balances, and free checking to everyone. "If you find these discriminatory practices happening, question the majority bank if there's not a minority bank in your community. You can effect change by asking questions. I always recommend writing letters to the bank president and expressing your concern if you see this happening," she says. "We need to do much more in our own interest."

THE LAST WORD

CHAPPELL SAYS THAT AFRICAN-AMERICANS NEED to be aware that we live in a capitalistic society where money is the common denominator. "There's always something to be done with money, particularly in the African-American community, because the need is so great. The time has come where we're going to have to give back and we have to have it in order to give it back. I believe in mentoring. I'm putting together a family foundation where I'd help bring along young people, who demonstrate math skills and who may be interested in a career in banking or finance," she says.

Chapter 3

Mark Winston Griffith is chairman of the board for Central Brooklyn Federal Credit Union. He received his B.A. from Brown University and M.A. from University of Ibadan in Nigeria. He currently resides in Brooklyn.

MARK WINSTON GRIFFITH

STARTING A CREDIT UNION FROM SCRATCH ISN'T AN easy task, but Mark Winston Griffith did it. He went from working in politics to becoming chairman of the board of the Central Brooklyn Federal Credit Union on Fulton Street in the heart of Bedford-Stuyvesant, New York, in just four years. With 6,000 members, it's the largest community development credit union in New York City.

"Considering how many members we have, our assets could be larger, but we serve a low- and moderate-income community and so logically what you get from that is low balances in people's accounts. Our assets are building, but it's going to require that we take in more members and offer higher dividends that will incentivize saving large amounts of money in the credit union," Griffith says. "We represent a financial cooperative that's in a low- and moderate-income neighborhood in the largest black community in the country that so far is surviving. This represents a high degree of success."

The $5.5-million institution was chartered in 1993, but it was started in 1989 as a result of a neighborhood-based effort. "We went to churches, we went to block parties, to block association meetings, and we got people to fill out pledges. We collected about 1,600 pledges and we took findings from the pledge forms and fed them into a business plan. We did five-year projections on how we would stay solvent. We put together a board of directors, a set of policies, and then we submitted a charter application to the National Credit Union Administration, which is a federal regulatory agency," Griffith says.

Once their application was approved, Griffith sent letters to the people who had filled out pledge forms and invited them to deposit their money. This stage took about two years. To help start the credit union, Griffith first established the Central Brooklyn Partnership, a community reinvestment organization, which helped pay expenses for the credit union until it turned a profit in 1995.

"Before we started the credit union, we realized that we needed an organization that would be separate from the credit union that would help support the credit union and would start other things. So before the union was even started, we had a revolving loan fund that was capitalized by the New York State Urban Development Corporation," he says. "I'm not on staff at the institution. I'm the chairman of the board and cofounder, but I serve on a board level, which is a volunteer position. Credit unions are all not-for-profit and all board service is noncompensated. My salary comes from the not-for-profit sponsoring organization, the Central Brooklyn Partnership."

The Partnership received grants from foundations, which is how all of the business's overhead expenses were paid. The Partnership works with the credit union membership, advocating on behalf of community reinvestment. Griffith still serves as the executive director of the Partnership.

"Our first office was right across the street. We then moved to another office building in the Bedford-Stuyvesant Restoration Plaza. Then a bank moved out of the neighborhood and they donated the building to us, which is where we are now on Fulton Street," he says. "It wasn't until we started making loans and charging fees on our deposits that we were able to generate revenue through the credit union independent of the Partnership.

"There are three ways in which the credit union makes revenues. A third of it comes from investments in other kinds of financial institutions, such as other banks and credit unions, mostly in CDs or government bonds. The second way is through fees we charge, including membership checking accounts, savings accounts, and money orders—different things that we offer. The third way is through interest on loans. But we were subsidized the first couple of years," he says. "The first time we turned a profit without being subsidized was 1995."

Although Griffith attended Ivy League schools and could probably land a high-paying position on Wall Street, he's chosen to serve the local community. He says that he's most interested in low- and moderate-income people because they have the least access to wealth-building information.

FINANCIAL ADVICE: ESTABLISH CREDIT

"I'd advise people to establish credit, and the way to do that is in a slow and basic, methodical way. Go to places like credit unions that offer good opportunities," he says. "Credit unions offer low-interest credit to people who may be considered high credit risks. Rates are lower through a credit union, but you should never try to get credit for something you don't have enough money for. Before you borrow, you have to be able to project what it's going to take to pay that loan back, and you have to take into account what your current income is, and possible emergency reserves you need."

Griffith says there are two types of loans that you can get from a credit union: share-secured loans and unsecured loans. A share-secured loan is a way to borrow against what you've already saved. If you have a thousand dollars on deposit, you can borrow against it. It's similar to having a secured credit card. For an unsecured loan, you have to have at least 10% of what you borrow on deposit.

"As soon as you enter adult life, start establishing credit. The best time is when you are self-sufficient, after college, or after getting a job. The idea behind establishing credit is you are establishing a good record that other people recognize and can be used for your future. The better credit you have, the easier it is to establish more credit and the cheaper it will be for you to get credit, as well," he says. "Credit is about proving to people that you pay your bills on time and that you're trustworthy."

Too often, people overextend themselves by attempting to purchase something that is beyond their means. Griffith advises reaching for what's within your balance by taking out a loan for something that's necessary and affordable, such as a car or computer. For example, Griffith himself went to another credit union and requested a $3,000 loan to buy a computer. Instead, he was offered $2,500. He took the money and since then has made every payment on time so that the next time he needs a loan, he can return and borrow a larger sum in an unsecured way. "You have to build relationships. That's what credit is about. I wouldn't start from 'I see a stereo; I want it.' I would start from 'I want to establish some credit; what is it that I could use right now that's relatively affordable and that wouldn't put me that far out in terms of credit?' "

He is also a strong advocate of the mantra "pay yourself first." "You have to figure out what your values are and what is most important to you and start putting money towards that. If your future is most important to you, or your health, then you should be putting money towards that every time you receive money," he says.

Griffith says the single most important investment that he's still reaping benefits from is a $3,000 certificate of deposit (CD) that was paying about 4% interest in 1994 from his credit union. "I took out a loan against it for 7% and was able to buy my first car. I was able to establish credit, which helped me to get credit at another credit union, which enabled me to get a Macy's credit card and an American Express charge card," he says. "I'm not an investment tycoon. I don't play the stock market and I don't take big gambles, because I have a modest income. So, I make a little bit of money and I invest it in short-, intermediate-, and long-term investments, and some things pay more than others. But I don't do anything high-risk."

PERSONAL PORTFOLIO

Griffith's personal portfolio is modest and conservative. It includes two CDs for a total of $6,000, an IRA, a life insurance policy, and an investment in Van Kampen American Capital Equity Opportunity Trust, a unit investment trust. "I track my money very closely. I use Quicken and I do everything on-line. I know where every penny goes. You can say that I budget my money. I put a little away every time I receive my paycheck, about 10%," he says. "I'm increasing my level of risk a little bit at a time. The older I get, the more capital I have to work with and the more I increase the risk within my portfolio. I save where I borrow, in my credit union. Once I save a certain amount, I then put it in a CD.

"CDs should not be your investment portfolio. They allow you to amass capital. You need to start off with CDs and work from there. A CD is a safe place to keep your money while you figure out what to do with it," he says. "It's not an investment goal. It's a vehicle for a less conservative investment. I haven't amassed enough to hit the second level, which is the riskier stuff—the mutual funds, the stocks."

Griffith says that African-Americans need to be conscious about what they are doing with their money. He advises that they pay attention to not only the return on their money but also what their money is supporting.

"I put my money in credit unions because I like the purpose, what the money is being used to do. I like the community development goal and mission that credit unions have," he says. "For people who don't have a lot of

---

CERTIFICATES OF DEPOSIT

CDs are timed deposits, says Thomas Clark, president and CEO of the Carver Federal Savings Bank, the largest African-American managed financial institution in the country.

"You can opt for a maturity of 30 days, 60 days, 90 days, or all the way up to 7 years," Clark says. The minimum investment is $500 and although there is no maximum, Clark states the Federal Deposit Insurance Corporation (FDIC) will only insure a CD up to $100,000.

The advantage of investing in a CD is that you get a fixed rate of return. However, you may run into trouble if you withdraw before maturity. "If you withdraw prior to the maturity, you pay a penalty. You forfeit the interest," Clark says.

Clark also gave an example of how a CD works. At Carver Federal Savings Bank, as of May 21, 1996, if you invested $2500 for 90 to 180 days, you'd receive an interest rate of 3.75% and an annual yield of 3.82%. Annual yield is the compounding rate.

disposable income, you need to control your money. Know where every penny is coming from and going to. Use a computer program that helps you manage your money and budget it. Using a computer enables you to stay on top of paying bills, and helps you track investments. I use Quicken. You can do anything with the right computer software."

Griffith says that many African-Americans start their own small businesses in order to gain control of their financial futures. However, he thinks starting a small business is not a good idea unless you have disposable income.

"Starting a small business is the riskiest venture you ever can undertake, and the vast majority ultimately fail. People initially start a business because they feel they can then be their own master. They won't have to report to a boss. They think they'll get rich. But, in reality, most small businesspeople are slaves to their business and they work harder than anyone else I know. I'm talking about small retail and wholesale operations, or sole proprietorship," he says. "If you start a business, you have to plan and know what you are doing. You have to make more money than you spend, or you get into trouble. I think people should be very cautious. Do research and get technical assistance from small business centers across the country. Don't try to start it on credit, because you'll be in a deeper hole than when you started if the business fails. Start your business at home and then expand it gradually."

A better way to a solid financial future is through self-education, Griffith says. "Invest towards retirement. The younger you start, the better. I'd do research on money management by picking up books. Go to the bookstore and do some reading. If there is someone who manages money that you trust, have a meeting with them. But don't give them all your money. Give them a small amount of money and see what they do with that. Be conservative in the beginning," he says.

INVESTING ADVICE: LOOK TO THE FUTURE

Griffith says the way you would plan your life should be the way you plan your financial future. "Put down on paper what's important to you, and where you want to be in a year, 5 years, 10 years, and 20 years. That's what should guide any investment decision. It depends on what your values are and what you want to do in life. But, always put something away for the long term, whether it's in an IRA or life insurance policy so that you'll have something no matter what else happens. Then, put something away for the short term," he says.

With $50 a month to invest, Griffith is conservative. He recommends putting money into a savings account until you have saved enough to put it in a CD. "Once you've raised five thousand dollars, start thinking about some less conservative financial options. Take a portion of that money and invest in something such as a mutual fund. I wouldn't recommend stocks unless you can stay on top of them," he says. "Ask around for recommendations for a trustworthy broker."

Griffith says avoid risky investments. "Don't start off with risky ventures. Start conservatively and work incrementally toward higher risk. Be very careful of stocks or anything you don't know much about. Before you put money in a mutual fund, find out what it is. If you are going to hook up with a broker, try to do it with a referral so that someone you know can vouch for the person. Watch out for small businesses unless you have disposable income, and stay away from venture capital investments, which is about taking an equity stake in a start-up business," he says.

THE LAST WORD

PAY YOUR BILLS ELECTRONICALLY. GRIFFITH SAYS that before he started paying bills on-line, he only made payments on a sporadic basis. "You can find out when your checks clear, and categorize them in different ways. It's also convenient. You don't pay for anything. With a couple of strokes of your finger, you can send out all of your bills at the same time. There's no muss, no fuss, no envelopes to lick, no stamps to lick," he says. "It happens at the same time every month. It makes it fun and interesting. Before, I'd deal with each bill separately and haphazardly. I saw it as a laborious and boring task and I always put it off until the last minute. Now, I just click in and execute my monthly transaction. Anytime you can make something like that fun, you are way ahead of the game."

Chapter 4

PAUL HUDSON

Paul C. Hudson is the president and CEO of Broadway
Federal Bank. He received his B.A. from the University
of California at Berkeley and J.D. from Boalt Hall School
of Law. He resides in Los Angeles, California,
with his wife and daughter.

BROADWAY FEDERAL BANK, BASED IN LOS ANGELES, IS
one of 11 black publicly traded companies and one of
two black banks that are publicly traded. It serves about
12,000 low-to-moderate-income customers in South Central Los Angeles and has $114 million in assets, with a $13
million net worth. The institution went public in January
of 1996. Paul Hudson has been president and CEO since
1992.

The 48-year-old grew up in South Central Los Angeles. He represents the third generation of his family to lead
Broadway Federal, the oldest black-owned thrift west of
the Mississippi River. His grandfather helped start the
thrift back in 1946 and his father was CEO before him.
The institution is at the mercy of the community it

serves. Its original building was burned down in the 1992 riots after the Rodney King verdict. But the financial institution kept going.

"It's an African-American–run business in an African-American community and I think it will create wealth for our community. It'll create jobs, and value for its investors, and it will recycle the dollars in our community through contracts with vendors, through employees' paychecks when they buy things in the community—and we hire people from the community. The time I'm investing growing this business will accrue to the benefit and the future of the African-American community," he says.

Broadway had an advantage when it went public, Hudson says, because it was not a new business starting up. The institution had been in operation for over 45 years and had built up retained earnings. As a result, it was an easier transaction to sell to the public.

"Our company was valued at $6.5 million and we raised $14 million. We ended up closing the transaction at $8.9 million and returned $5 million. Basically, we were oversubscribed, so we had to return some money to people who wanted shares but we just didn't have the shares to sell them. In that sense, it was very successful. We sold shares for $10 and we structured the transaction so that you could get in with a minimum of $250, which is a low threshold," he says. "We designed it that way so small investors could get into the transaction. A lot of our investors are first-time investors in the stock market or lower-income folk, so we tried to make it affordable."

About a year ago, Broadway stock was trading at $10.75 and paying a 2% annual dividend. "I bought shares when everyone else bought shares. I bought a little over six thousand shares," he says. "There are dividends and there's also appreciated value of the stock. I think my investment in the company is my belief that it will go even higher than $10.75. That's about 75% of what the company's worth. If it was liquidated today, the stock would be worth about $14 a share. So, it's undervalued. As an investment, I stand to make a 40% return, in addition to the dividends, if the stock goes up to $14 a share."

This is the type of investment opportunity that African-Americans should look for. However, Hudson says it's difficult for African-Americans to save and accumulate wealth in a society that still makes distinctions based on race. He believes that the savings rate of African-Americans is too low. "That's probably as a result of our putting too much emphasis on current gratification or immediate satisfaction—for example, 'I need this color TV even though I already have a good black-and-white one.' That's stuff that's immediately nice but over the long term doesn't provide security for your family or community," he says. "The biggest problem is that African-Americans have an inability to save and accumulate wealth because of a variety of issues.

"One issue is that black people don't make as much money as the majority community when they have jobs. They have a higher unemployment rate, and their exposure to investment opportunities is considerably less. So, even if they have accumulated savings, their investment portfolios tend to yield a lower rate of return than people with greater financial sophistication. That's kind of a vicious circle. We have to understand that a large part of wealth comes from inheritance. Wealth from generation to generation begins to compound."

PERSONAL PORTFOLIO

Hudson recommends saving 10% of your gross income. Hudson himself, however, saves only between 3% and 6%. His largest single investment is in the bank and that's because he believes in its future success. "My belief is that if the business prospers, I'll prosper. It's a strategy or belief that if I put a lot of time into the bank and the bank's future, then I will reap rewards both personally and financially," he says.

Aside from owning shares in Broadway Federal, Hudson has also invested in some real estate. "I invested a lot in my home and I have some rental units. I have a lot invested in my retirement accounts through the bank that I personally set aside. I'm invested in other stocks through mutual funds in my 401(k) plan," he says. "I believe in diversification. That is, I don't put all my eggs in one basket. As you can see, there's some real estate, and there's my 401(k)—which is invested one-third aggressively, one-third balanced (equities and fixed-income instruments), and one-third in a conservative money market account. The riskiest investment is my investment in the bank, and that has a big growth potential. My retirement funds are invested kind of balanced over the investment spectrum."

Hudson estimates his net worth to be somewhere between $400,000 and $500,000. He attributes his personal fortune to saving and investing in real estate at the early age of 30. Hudson started saving by putting up to $1,500 a year in an IRA when he was 25 years old because of the tax benefits. "If I could have done it earlier, I would have been better off," he says. "I think that even if you're not an aggressive investor, if you start investing and saving early it's very hard not to accumulate wealth—if you do it on a consistent basis. I haven't done it on a consistent basis and I'm better off than the average citizen. So if you do it consistently, you could really do well."

He believes investing in IRAs is one key to amassing a large personal fortune. "I believe in saving, and secondly, there were the tax advantages at the time of the IRA. So, I was trying to shelter income and trying to save at the same time. The attractive thing about IRAs is you get penalties if you take the money out, which motivates you to leave the money alone. I still think it's a sound strategy even though the tax advantages aren't as good now," he says.

The other key to amassing a fortune was his investment in real estate. "When I invested in middle-income properties, it was a lot more attractive than it is today, but I still think it's a good investment. As long as you don't mind managing property, I think it's a sound investment."

Hudson calls himself a conservative investor. He says the perfect asset allocation is 10% in cash, savings, and money market accounts; 25% in real estate; 25% in fixed-income instruments; and the balance of 40% in equities.

"It's diversified, so if the market tanks or real estate goes down, your whole portfolio is not going to be affected. You've got between 20% and 25% in very conservative investments that won't ride up or down real fast. It's a balanced portfolio that gives you more even returns over the long term, but it lets you also ride upturns in equities and the real estate market, which I think are the ones that have the greatest risk and the greatest reward," he says.

He adds that it's almost impossible to net 10% to 12% returns unless you become an active investor. "Getting up to 12% returns means that you're not going to be a weekend investor. It means you're going to work at investments," he says. "There are different types of investors. There are people who let others do the investing for them through mutual funds, or through the advice of friends or a stockbroker. Those are people who don't want to take the time to evaluate their own investments. They just kind of want a balanced portfolio. They want to put the money away and not have to worry about it. There's a chance you'll get 10% investing like that. To ensure that you get 10% to 12%, you have to be an active investor. That means you have to do your homework. You have to evaluate the investment. Then you can make 10% in real estate, and you can make 10% in equities or almost any type of investment. Generally, it's very difficult to get double-digit returns. Most people have gotten those returns in the market, but this has been an unusually high market. On average, 10% in the market is a good return over the long term."

In order to control their financial futures, Hudson says African-Americans need to accumulate wealth through saving and investing. "There are lots of books on the lack of wealth among African-Americans. We don't have large net assets. For me to have a $400,000 net worth, that's not a lot. I'm embarrassed at how low that is. I tend to rationalize my low net worth by saying that I'm building a business that will live beyond me and have a benefit for my community beyond me," he says. "African-Americans are really not at the table in terms of wealth, and we should be. To control our futures, we have to be [at the table]. It goes back to how we invest, whether we invest our money in cars, televisions, and clothes or whether we invest our money in real estate, stocks, and companies."

INVESTING ADVICE: MIDDLE OF THE ROAD WITH A LITTLE GAMBLING

With a hypothetical $50,000 inheritance, Hudson said investing would depend on age. But generally, he would select a middle-of-the-road investment strategy that seeks above-market returns. "I'd advise them to put 10% in a CD, 50% into an equity growth fund, 30% into a more conservative balanced fund that invests equally between fixed-income securities and blue-chip stocks, and with the remaining 10% or five thousand dollars I'd try to hit that home run. I'd do my homework and see if there's a stock or real estate investment that's a sleeper. I'd look for above-market returns with that five thousand dollars, kind of like a gamble," he says.

For those who can afford to save or invest only $50 a month, Hudson recommends opening a savings account and starting an investment club. "The most conservative thing you can do is put $50 in an interest-bearing savings account, like a passbook account where you'd earn 2% to 3% a year. But you're better off investing with a group of people. If everybody is putting in $50 a month and you have six people, then you're really doing $300," he says. "There are a variety of strategies the group can implement, rather than using a savings account. But the key is first to save, even at $50 a month, because you can't participate in the investment market without some cash reserves."

Although Hudson is in favor of garnering high returns, he says to be wary of investments that promise 30% returns and above. "Someone may come to you and say, 'I can make a 100% return on your investment.' That's when your protective defenses should go up. I firmly believe that making money is a slow, tedious process. There aren't a lot of ways that you can make money fast. I would advise people to be patient. There are no get-rich-quick schemes that I could recommend."

THE LAST WORD

"**O**NCE YOU GET $100,000 YOU CAN HAVE THE DIVER-sified portfolio that I recommended. If every African-American could shoot for that goal, it'd be great. Look for opportunities in your employer's 401(k) plan. Leverage your dollar by buying a $100,000 house with $10,000. You can also look into forming an investment club," Hudson says. "Realistically, on a $30,000 salary, saving 10% a year is about $3,000. With interest, in 10 years or less you'll have $100,000, but you shouldn't go out and buy a Mercedes with that $100,000."

Hudson believes that African-Americans need to trust each other enough to come together and pool resources in mergers and investment clubs, because they generate higher returns quicker. "People can understand when you talk about investment clubs, but even those are difficult for African-Americans to put together and trust enough to join them and stay together. Take that to the next level of two sophisticated businesses coming together and trusting each other enough. The effect is the same. If we pool our resources we can grow faster and generate above-market returns. As African-Americans we need to elevate our level of trust, especially when people have limited income and don't have a big inheritance to draw on. The strategy that we ought to begin to explore is trusting each other enough to pool our resources," he says.

Chapter 5

Frank Savage is chairman of Alliance Capital Management International. He received his B.A. from Howard University and M.A. from Johns Hopkins School of Advanced International Studies. He currently resides in Stamford, Connecticut, with his wife and six children.

FRANK SAVAGE

FRANK SAVAGE IS CHAIRMAN OF ALLIANCE CAPITAL Management International, which means that he's instrumental in setting up joint ventures, establishing offices overseas, and creating partnerships with other countries and new investment vehicles so that Americans can invest outside the United States. He is also on the board of directors of Alliance Capital Management, the parent company of Alliance Capital International.

Prior to his current position, he was chairman of Equitable Capital Management, which merged with Alliance Capital in 1993. Savage started his finance career with Citibank in the international division straight out of graduate school. He worked in New York, Saudi Arabia, and Liberia as part of the management group running the Citibank branches.

"I've been a banker or involved in securities investing all of my life, and now I'm more involved in the leadership of the company—in mapping the strategy and guiding the business. But I draw on all the experience that I got over the years in investing. I think the way to be successful is you need to know the basics," he says.

Although Savage knew that he would pursue an international career, he didn't know about the financial services industry until his second year at Johns Hopkins University, where he was studying for a master's degree in international relations. "The only career path I could foresee internationally was with the foreign service. I didn't see a business option. But, when I graduated with my master's in 1968, I got opportunities to talk to banks and oil companies. I started getting opportunities to join these global organizations," he says.

PERSONAL PORTFOLIO

Savage's own portfolio is highly diversified. He's invested in communications, computer technology, finance, and minerals. "The important thing is to diversify. I try to identify those sectors that I think will grow rapidly. I'm a growth stock investor. I'm not interested in companies that are just going to pay modest dividends at every quarter. I like to invest in companies where I buy in at $30 and it's going to be worth $120 in a few years," he says.

INVESTING ADVICE: INVEST FOR COLLEGE— AND OVERSEAS

Savage commented on Alliance Capital's Financial Preparedness Study, which found that 53% of African-Americans are putting money aside for their children's college education compared to 46% of whites. The poll, conducted by Louis Harris & Associates, also found that African-Americans begin saving earlier for their children's education. African-Americans start saving when their children are at an average age of 6.7 years old compared to 9 years old for whites.

"African-Americans tend to be saving for college for their children much earlier than the population at large, and this is clearly indicative of the importance that African-American families attach to a college education," Savage says. "On average African-Americans make a lot less than the population at large, so if they want to save money to cover the first four years [of higher education], they have to start early because they have a smaller revenue base to work from. It makes sense that they would start at an earlier age. In African-American families, education has always been seen as the most important thing for kids, and it's seen as an absolute prerequisite to be successful in this competitive and problematic society for minorities."

Savage says that "early" is as soon as the child is born. "The earlier you start the better off you are," he says. He used savings bonds, investments in individual stocks, mutual funds, and his income to put all three of his kids through college. He also dipped into his 401(k) plan.

"You have 17 years to invest. If you invest in the equity market and get a market return, you could do extremely well. And, you can invest for the long term, which means this is not money you'll be taking out for household things. You could put your money into fixed-income securities or equities. We feel that mutual funds are the way to go, because you're setting aside small amounts. You get the benefit of pooling money of several people in one vehicle, and you'll get topflight investment management that ordinarily would not be available to an individual investor. You also get timely reporting, so you know exactly what's happening in the account. You can track it. Mutual funds are the most efficient way to invest for this type of purpose," he says.

According to Savage, the first thing to do is to find out how much a college education is going to cost; then start putting away incremental amounts to meet that need. In other words, come up with a plan based on what the family can afford to invest. If you invest on a regular basis for 17 years, you won't have to pay out as much when the child comes of age and is ready for college. In addition to investing on a regular basis, Savage recommends diversifying among stocks, bonds, and real estate.

"Invest on a regular basis—that way it doesn't hurt as much. It's difficult to come up with a number for how much to save and invest a month. The number has to be a function of your family's financial situation. But, in general, you should contribute until it hurts, because you want to make sure the child has funds available to cover college expenses when they come due. Some people may invest in zero-coupon bonds or Treasury strip bonds," he says.

In addition to investing for college, Savage's expertise lies in international investing. He just helped launch a mutual fund to invest in Egypt and established a joint venture with an Egyptian bank.

"I'm involved in creating new investment vehicles for people to be able to invest in markets outside the United States. We have to be very creative in how we establish these. We can't just go in and open an office. For example, when you go to Eastern Europe you want to set up a partnership with a local institution, because the most important thing in investing in emerging markets is to have local knowledge. So we set up a partnership or joint venture with a local financial institution and we offer our services to the local market base through that joint venture," he says.

When investing outside the United States, the most important thing is to be diversified. For stable returns similar to U.S. market returns, Savage advises investing in Europe and Japan through mutual funds. "You'll get a good return, and on a risk-adjusted basis it will be a very attractive return, because those markets are closer to the United States. As a U.S. investor you want to have the majority of your money invested domestically. But you want to diversify, because there are opportunities to get good returns on a safe basis outside the country. You don't want to put money in any one area—you may want to put some of it in Europe, Asia, and Middle Eastern Africa and some of it in Latin America," he says.

Within investing internationally, Savage says that emerging markets are very attractive. They include countries such as Poland, Egypt, South Africa, Brazil, Argentina, Russia, and the Philippines. "Everyone is moving toward market-driven economies, and everyone is moving toward some form of democracy. So, you don't have the kind of political risk that you used to have during the Cold War. I call it the 'peace dividend,' which means that all of these new countries are now unlocking the entrepreneurial and business potential of their people. They are creating stock markets and bond markets, and removing exchange controls. They are becoming investor-friendly. They offer an opportunity to take advantage of some of the really positive economic changes taking place in these countries," he says.

Before jumping into emerging markets, Savage recommends considering your risk profile. He says people should have 15% to 20% of their assets invested internationally, and 5% of that amount should be invested in emerging markets.

Savage says the most important investment he's made that he's still reaping benefits from is his investment in Alliance, his own company. He recommends investing in what you know and one way to do that is by investing in the company you work for. "If you are working in a significant position in a company, invest in your own company, because you know the company," he says. "Try to invest close to home."

He is invested in a slew of Alliance mutual funds, including the Alliance International Fund, the European Fund, the Growth Stock Fund, and the Southern Africa Fund, and in some special industry funds, such as health care.

Savage also invests in the companies where he is a director. He sits on the board of directors of Essence Communications, ARCO Chemical Company, Lockheed Martin Corporation, and the Council on Foreign Relations.

THE LAST WORD

IF THERE'S ONE THING SAVAGE WANTS AFRICAN-Americans to know, it is that there's tremendous opportunity in the international area. "Americans in general are not as active international investors as people in other parts of the world, but increasingly more money is going international. It's an area to look at because there's opportunity to invest in some very attractive markets, and most importantly you don't have the same type of political risk that you had during the Cold War era," he says.

When asked whether African-Americans should give preferential treatment to African nations because they are black, Savage says to invest first to help yourself. "If someone wants to assist in what's happening in Russia, South Africa, or Asia, that's a personal decision. I would never suggest that African-Americans should invest in Africa. But people who are invested in our Southern Africa Fund feel good about the fact that they are helping South Africa to achieve its goals, plus they are making a nice return, and that's the perfect situation. You should make either an investment decision or a social decision," he says. "I happen to invest in the Southern Africa Fund because I knew I'd get a good return and secondly because I wanted to be part of that process of change. But that's a highly personal decision."

In order to successfully invest internationally, Savage recommends doing research on international markets in order to get a general sense of what's going on in these countries. His motto is to become aware.

Some places to look include CNN, the BBC, and the French Channel. Savage also says to read the *Financial Times*, the *Wall Street Journal*, *Barron's*, and *Forbes*, all of which have international coverage. "A constant intake of knowledge through reading is very important, because these markets are dynamic. Things are changing all the time. If you're not reading and being aware on a continual basis, you'll be out of the loop. So, you have to make a special effort by reading and listening to television," he says.

The pitfalls of investing internationally are the same as investing domestically. "The biggest difference is that sometimes the macroeconomic management of these countries can deviate from what you expected, and that can ripple through to the stock and bond market. The same thing can happen in the United States, but with international trends, you are further away from the countries. This is why it's important to invest in mutual funds so that you get the benefit of experts who are on top of these markets," Savage says. "If you go out and buy international stocks on your own, you will not be on top of the latest developments."

Part III

FINANCIAL PLANNING

Chapter 6

Rozlyn Anderson is managing director of The Chase Manhattan Private Bank. She received her B.A. from Harvard/Radcliffe and J.D. from Harvard Law School. She currently resides in Montclair, New Jersey, with her husband and two children.

ROZLYN ANDERSON

ROZLYN ANDERSON, MANAGING DIRECTOR AT THE Chase Manhattan Bank, has worked with the bank for seven years. Prior to that she practiced law for 10 years in the fields of tax and trusts and estates. Her areas of expertise are business succession planning and estate planning.

"The great satisfaction I derive is from helping clients discern their needs and helping them come up with solutions to their financial issues," she says. "Prior to joining the bank I was in private practice, so many of my clients came through that avenue. Some came from referrals through friends and some were clients of the law firms. Now that I've joined the bank, I work primarily with the clients of the private bank and our middle market, which is the commercial lending area."

Anderson deals with ultrahigh net worth individuals whose assets range from $3 million to $1 billion. She defines estate planning as a lifelong exercise or the orderly transfer of one's assets both during lifetime and after one's death with the hope of minimizing taxes so there are sufficient assets left for survivors.

Regardless of the size of your assets, Anderson says that estate planning is a self-discovery process. "It's enormously illuminating and something that everyone should do. Understand your assets and liabilities and the tax implications of various forms of ownership and strategies that can be employed," she says.

African-American clients are no different from any other ethnic group in that they need some sort of a will. Administering an estate with no will is more expensive, Anderson says, because the courts have to get involved in appointing administrators, which can lead to expense and delays. Anderson advises anyone over the age of 18 to have a will.

ESTATE PLANNING

"I think that overall estate planning is good because it lets people focus and do basic financial planning. People often start a discussion about estate planning and realize they need to better organize their overall finances when they discover how assets can be dispersed as part of a plan or through lifetime giving. The average person needs a will, but the vast majority of people don't have them. In the absence of a will, state laws will determine how one's assets are passed along. If you have minor children, it's important to have a will to express who should be the guardian in the event neither parent survives," she says.

"The problem is that in most states in the United States, the legislature has determined that a certain percentage of assets will go to the spouse and a certain percentage will go to children. And in many cases, I have found that that is not the person's real desire. From a tax standpoint, it is inefficient. If someone has assets in excess of $600,000, it's possible it will generate a tax if all the assets do not go to the spouse. In many cases, people prefer the spouse to get the entire amount of assets. The important thing is to focus on what are the desires. I would not like to see people be automatically subject to statutes without contemplating the situation."

Prior to writing a will, it's important to have a notion of what assets you have, what the ownership of those assets is, what rights you have to pension assets, and the income tax and estate tax effects of holding onto the assets. Anderson says people do a lot of inefficient planning by failing to look carefully at the ownership of the asset, and by failing to look at beneficiary designations where assets could be controlled by a designation outside the will.

"You need to understand what titling means, whether one should hold assets in one's own name or jointly between spouses. That's extremely important, but it depends on the circumstances. Families with more than $1.2 million in assets have to be careful to have at least $625,000 in each spouse's name, because federal law gives a $625,000 tax exemption in 1998 to each person. If all assets are in one spouse's name and the other spouse dies first, then you've lost the ability to take advantage of that spouse's exemption. So, ownership is extremely important. Many couples think it's romantic to hold assets jointly, but it isn't always the best practice from the standpoint of taxes and estate planning."

An alternative to drawing up a will is setting up a living trust, which acts as a will substitute. One advantage to a living trust is that it doesn't have to pass through probate court, which can be onerous. "It provides a certain degree of confidentiality whereas once wills are filed in probate, they can be accessed by the public. Trust documents will eventually become public, but it will take a long time. Some people say there's less cost in administering an estate with a trust. Also, if there might be a will contest in the family, it might be advisable to use a trust, although trusts can be contested as well," she says.

Anderson says that land ownership affects many African-Americans who have inherited land from their ancestors. Whether to sell or hold the land depends on certain factors. Anderson says you should make the determination based on your needs and goals with respect to your other assets.

"From a symbolic standpoint, land is what African-American families were promised after Reconstruction, and some families still have that land legacy. In my case, members of my family earned money and were able to purchase part of the original plantation lands in Virginia. This land is something we will always want to hold in our family. There are emotional reasons to hold onto certain assets that are not necessarily the best financial reasons. African-Americans need proper advice on the ownership and disposition of the lands and perhaps even development of the land," she says. "We have family farmland in Florida, and the issue now is whether to sell off the lots and actually have the land developed. There's a psychological and emotional pull. The intellectual analysis of the land is that it's not being farmed. It's not producing sufficient income. It's a drain on my grandmother's assets, so we are investigating developing the land so that it will become income-producing. Many African-American families are in this position. My advice is don't let the symbolic, emotional, and psychological aspects of holding onto the land cloud your judgment when it comes to the needs of the family. If there are significant income needs, then you have to look at ways to make this an income-producing property."

Anderson says that people should decide what their life's goals are very early. "If one is going to retire or perhaps cease one career and shift to another or start a business, those goals need to be figured out and then you have to plan for them. We've devised some proprietary software for clients where we will help them look over their life span and life events and determine how much they should be investing, what kind of return they need to seek in order to accomplish their goals within a given time period that they've set for themselves," she says. "So, starting with goals first is extremely important, followed by looking at one's overall asset picture and seeing how various assets can be leveraged to achieve the goals. Make sure the goals are realistic. Our computer model tells clients whether their goals are realistic."

In her work, Anderson has found that some of the wealthiest Americans, such as Warren Buffett and Bill Gates, don't want their children to receive the lion's share of their wealth. Instead, they think their own children should work hard to amass wealth. Wealthy people often opt to devote some of their money to charity. Anderson says that African-American families need to decide whether they want to pass on a certain amount of wealth to their children and also pursue charitable goals. Charitable gifts can be lifetime gifts or outright gifts, or they can be structured in trust. There are such things as the charitable split-interest trust where you can retain the income for life or provide that it go to another person and the remainder of the trust would go to charity. There are significant tax advantages to that type of structure.

"There are significant tax advantages to making gifts to charity," she says. "I think that many African-Americans who have achieved a measure of success are concerned about how they might give back to the community. This is one way financially that they can express their appreciation for their achievements and also give back to the community in a way they feel is meaningful."

Anderson recommends putting property into partnership structures. "Then to pass on shares in partnerships, particularly limited partnership shares, is one way of taking advantage of discounts, which can be anywhere from 30% to 50%. If you just give somebody a piece of land outright, there's no discount. But, if you first put that land into a partnership (there are no tax consequences for contributing it to the partnership), and then you give your child a limited partnership interest in that partnership, you will be able to get a discount for making that gift. By passing on that property, you are getting it out of your estate and you're getting the appreciation in that property out of your estate," she says.

"The great thing about family limited partnerships," says Anderson, "is that the parent retains the title of general partner and can control the use and disposition of the land even while giving limited partnership interest to the children. In the ideal situation, the parent keeps 1% interest as a partner but will give the other 99% of limited partnership interest to the next generation. They've been able to use their annual exclusion of $10,000 per person and it's a way of using the discounts to transfer property in excess of that $10,000. To do this, you have to contact a lawyer and an outside appraiser to get the property appraised and determine what the discount should be, because the IRS might challenge the magnitude of the discount. The IRS is quite wise to the fact that these are very popular devices."

In talking about the IRS, Anderson says there must be a business purpose for setting up the partnership. It cannot have a tax avoidance purpose. "It's more questionable as to whether you can use this partnership structure for cash and marketable securities. Seek opinion of counsel before you set something up," she says. "Ask for a discount of 50%. Some have argued for 70% to 80%, but that's inviting an audit. It can be done tax-free if one takes advantage of the $10,000 annual gift tax exclusion (which will be indexed to inflation in 1999), or the $625,000 lifetime exemption."

FINANCIAL ADVICE: BE MINDFUL OF TAX LAWS AND FORM OF OWNERSHIP

The pitfalls of estate planning include inattention to tax laws and inattention to form of ownership, Anderson says. In both cases, you can lose money to the IRS. A perfect example is life insurance ownership. "Take, for example, owning a $500,000 insurance policy in your own name. When you die, the amount is included in estate tax purposes, which bumps up the size of the estate by $500,000. Essentially, Uncle Sam is getting about $250,000 of the $500,000. The way to avoid that is to put it in a life insurance trust. Before acquiring the policy, have the trust set up and then the trustee of the trust makes the application. The trust becomes the owner and the beneficiary. It's a wonderful benefit because you avoid bumping up the size of the estate," she says. "Few people realize how much they are worth when they die because they forget to include the value of the life insurance that they own in their own name. After $625,000, the IRS starts taxing your estate at 37% and can go up to 55%. That's why business owners say Uncle Sam is the silent partner. The person who should be most concerned about this is a person with illiquid assets, such as real estate, or a business, where there isn't a ready market. Many of these people have to look into other funding structures like insurance to be able to meet that tax so that the family is not forced to sell the land or the business in order to pay the taxes—because they're due nine months after death."

Many African-Americans aspire to be wealthy, but they don't realize that there is a cost to that status. Anderson says it's important to be mindful of the responsibilities of wealth. "Be aware that there's a system in place that's going to tax property whenever you attempt to transfer it, whether it be during your lifetime or after death. Understand the rules of the system and how you can cleverly take advantage of the system, because there are advantages written into the tax law that are accepted strategies to minimize some of the taxes. One is doing oneself a disservice not to be aware of those strategies," she says.

Anderson advises looking at your will every two years to keep up with rapid changes in the law. "There's a proposal being revived to exempt a certain percentage of the value of a family business, which will be important to many African-Americans. They need to work closely with lobbying groups that are looking out for their interests with respect to tax minimization."

THE LAST WORD

ANDERSON, WHO ATTENDED HARVARD/RADCLIFFE College and the Harvard Law School, says that it is critical for the future success of African-Americans to invest in the best education for their children. She believes that her education was the most important investment her parents and grandparents made for her. "When it comes to setting goals for lifetime planning, I would strongly suggest that the education of our children be built in. I have started planning for my children's education and looking for the most appropriate vehicles towards that goal," she says.

Chapter 7

Glinda Bridgforth is president and CEO of Bridgforth Financial Management Group. She received her B.S. from Western Michigan University. She currently resides in Oakland, California.

GLINDA BRIDGFORTH

LESS THAN A DECADE AGO, GLINDA BRIDGFORTH faced financial disaster and divorce. Fortunately, she found a way to deal with her situation, and now she's teaching her holistic approach to money management.

In 1989, Bridgforth, based in Oakland, California, was going through a divorce, had taken a leave of absence from her job as an executive at the Wells Fargo & Company bank, and was facing $50,000 in unsecured debt. To make matters worse, she had income property that was in foreclosure and the home she was living in was getting ready to go into foreclosure.

It didn't matter that she had been managing $90 million in assets for the bank where she was working. "Even though I had all of this responsibility and was successful in terms of managing the bank's money, my personal finances were out of control. I just went through what I call my life crisis. I found myself burnt out on banking, I was in a marriage that wasn't working, and my finances were out of control. I needed to take a step back and look at my life and what was going on. I decided to leave the bank, leave the marriage, and work on my finances," she says.

Bridgforth sought the support she needed to regroup emotionally, spiritually, and financially. "I came through all of that devastation. That's my financial success. I have paid off practically all of that debt, and now I have a lot to offer other people—because life has various kinds of circumstances that tend to happen, and we have no control over that. So, just being able to help people understand that they can overcome financial challenges and devastation is satisfying. It was not comfortable going through parts that were extremely painful, but to have rebuilt my life—and to be in a better position now than I have ever been—is the greatest success that I have."

Just one year after her crisis, Bridgforth started the Bridgforth Financial Management Group, a cash and debt management company. "I learned such a tremendous amount about dealing with this crisis, that I decided to teach this information to people," she says. "As I was going through this recovery process from the life crisis, I knew that I didn't want to go back into banking. I really felt that I had put in all of the time I needed to there. As I looked at all that I had come through and that I had gotten myself back on track, I then started to be encouraged by other individuals that I could share this information. I began the process of doing research. How valid is this business? Is there a market for it? Are there people who would pay for counseling for their finances? I started talking to people about the possibility of offering a financial consulting service. I became increasingly encouraged until I finally started building the business one client at a time."

In order to get clients, Bridgforth held seminars. "I would market and advertise the seminars. I did my own marketing and promotion, and that got me exposure, and then one thing led to another. I was being invited to various workshops and conferences, and I was being contacted to do television interviews and for print media. As a result, my client base grew," she says.

Bridgforth started the business with a couple of thousand dollars. There was little overhead because she was working from home. At the time of her divorce, she sold some real estate property—a duplex and a single-family home—that she owned, and she used the profits to live on while she built her business. Her 401(k) account also provided somewhat of a cushion.

"I paid off some bills and I had a plan. I knew that I

had to look at what my needs were going to be. I was able to determine how much I'd need on a monthly basis to live and how much money it would cost in order to initially get the business started. I considered the other assets I had available, in terms of retirement accounts and so forth," she says. "There was low overhead so it wasn't as though I needed to put a lot of money into the business. What I needed was enough money to support myself while my business grew. So the money I had set aside was used to supplement the income coming in from the business for the first two years. It's a service-oriented business. I offer a service. I'm paid an hourly fee. It's a pay-as-you-go business. So, I typically don't have receivables and that sort of thing. It's a very simple business to offer."

As a financial counselor, Bridgforth helps clients gain control of their finances by offering them a structured program so that they know how to deal with their finances on a day-to-day basis. Her clients make anywhere from $30,000 to $300,000. Bridgforth has about 200 clients at any given time. Her clients come in on a monthly basis for a six-month period.

"They are people who make good money but don't know where it's going. They feel they don't have enough to show for all of the money that they make. They feel that they should have more accumulated. My approach is holistic, which differentiates me from other financial counselors. I'm the step before the financial planner," she says. "I think it's important to sit down and identify what their issues and concerns are about their finances, and get an idea of their short-term goals, and to get a sense of what their money patterns have been. I have people bring in a list of their debts. We look at the balances, the monthly payments, and the interest rate, and then we determine the exact amount of the debt. After I get a sense of their money history, I do a cash flow analysis. We identify in detail what their needs are on a monthly basis."

In order to get a financial portrait of her clients, Bridgforth has people break down their spending to come up with a budget. She prefers to call this a "spending plan" because she says generally people are resistant to budgets. "I have people break down what they're spending in the grocery store or out in restaurants. We come up with a spending plan, which is the step before investing," she says. "We, as African-Americans, control about $400 billion a year in income. We have money but because of our spending patterns we feel it's all or nothing. Either we have money that we can put into investments or we just don't do anything. What I do is help people get control of that spending and help them accumulate money, and I refer them to investment advisers. I work with them to help them get ready to invest by helping them identify what their spending patterns are."

To identify your spending patterns, Bridgforth says you should start writing down all the money you spend daily and total it by category. "One of the most important things I've found when working with clients is that often they will modify their spending behavior automatically when they see in print the total amounts of money they are spending in different areas," she says. "For example, it's illuminating to add up the yearly cost of one's daily cappuccinos to find out it exceeds $1,200 annually."

Bridgforth says many African-Americans grew up with a poverty consciousness, which is causing them to spend all of their money. "What tends to happen with a lot of people is that there was so much deprivation when they were growing up that when they become adults and start making good money, they spend it as fast as it comes in because they're still trying to compensate for all the lack and scarcity that there was when they were children," she says.

To change someone's poverty consciousness, Bridgforth advocates an exercise called "Messages, Beliefs, Actions," which is about examining the negative message received in childhood and changing it into a positive belief system. "The exercise takes you from the message that you received to the belief system you've developed based on that message and then what action pattern you have developed as a result as an adult. If the action pattern is something that's detrimental to your financial well-being, then it needs to be changed. We then develop an affirmation that counters that belief," she says.

Bridgforth says that after developing a positive affirmation about money, she tells clients to write it down and put it where they can see it first thing in the morning. "I recommend that you meditate with it five or ten minutes in the morning and again at night before bed. It has a subconscious effect, and over time you begin to believe it and it counters that negative belief you had."

Bridgforth, a New Age guru and former bank executive, is proudest of her investment in personal growth and development, which includes therapy, support groups, and self-help activities such as books, classes, seminars, and workshops. "We function with a lot of baggage. It wasn't until I went through my life crisis and began to work with a therapist that I got in touch with what wasn't working in my life," she says. "I used to think that Wells Fargo bank was my source, but after going through the challenges that I did I began to realize that it was just a channel by which my good comes to me and so once I had recognized that, it was the beginning of a change."

THE FUNDAMENTALS OF THE HOLISTIC APPROACH TO MONEY MANAGEMENT

The Emotional Aspects: Examine belief system, history, and attitudes about money.

The Practical Skills: Consistently set goals, balance your checkbook, develop a spending plan, track your spending, and save money.

The Spiritual Side: Meditation, affirmation, and visualization.

EMOTIONAL MONEY INVENTORY *

1. Who handled the money in your home when you were growing up? What attitude did that person have about money (frivolous, generous, prudent, fearful, etc.)?
2. What type of relationship did you have with that person (good, bad, loving, angry, fearful, etc.)?
3. As a child, did you think you were rich or poor? Did you worry about having enough money?
4. When you were growing up, where did you get your money? Did it come from an allowance, gifts, jobs, or other source?
5. How old were you when you got your first job? How did you feel about it? What did you do with the money you earned?
6. Based on your responses to the above questions, what did you learn about money when you were growing up, and how does that message affect you as an adult?

*Source: Glinda F. Bridgforth, *The Basic Money Management Workbook*, Self-published. 1994, $20; to order 1-888-430-1820.

MESSAGES, BELIEFS, ACTIONS*

Example of the exercise:

Message from Childhood: Money means violence and/or death.
Resulting Belief Held: If I deal with money, I'll die.
Resulting Action Pattern: I gave complete control of our money to my spouse.
New Affirmation: I am confident and competent to handle money.

Source: Glinda F. Bridgforth, *The Basic Money Management Workbook*, Self-published. 1994, $20; to order 1-888-430-1820.

Still, Bridgforth acknowledges that the investments she made prior to her divorce and life crisis helped her situation. "I used the proceeds of my 401(k) plan to supplement my income while I started the business. Today, the potential of the business is greater than the income that I was making as a bank employee, and it's greater than the return that I gained from investments in real estate and the 401(k) account," she says.

Bridgforth says that personal growth is important because it provides the self-esteem necessary to carry on in case of emergencies. "You really need to grow so that you have confidence and belief in yourself no matter what happens. If you lose your job, you'll find another job or you'll be able to start a business and if that business fails, you'll be able to start another business," she says. "You also have to maintain a spiritual belief in a higher power because at times when circumstances get beyond your control, you need something to hang onto. When you have that, no

---

GLINDA'S FAVORITE MONEY AFFIRMATIONS

I am something to celebrate.

I confidently and competently handle my money.

All of my wants and needs are met because God is my source.

---

matter what happens, then you know that you'll make it through. You'll know that you are being divinely supported and guided."

PERSONAL PORTFOLIO

Bridgforth's approach to investing is less spiritual and more active. She invests in the Putnam Income and Growth Fund. She also has some stock holdings, including Air Touch Communications, a technology company, and Fort Howard, a paper company. She found Fort Howard through a broker who addressed her investment club. Air Touch Communications is a local company that she heard about through word of mouth.

She advocates dollar cost averaging as a way to maintain consistency. "I have an automatic transfer from my checking account to go into a savings account at a credit union. It's a place where my money can accumulate. The credit union account was paying a bit more interest than what the bank was paying. About $200 is transferred to the credit union and about $400 is transferred into my mutual fund on a monthly basis," she says. She also puts $50 a month into her investment club account.

"I dollar cost average because there's a tendency,

DOLLAR COST AND VALUE AVERAGING

Dollar cost averaging is a system of investing the same amount of money into the same investment vehicle, whether it be a mutual fund or savings account. With a mutual fund, the result is that you buy more shares when the price is lower and fewer shares when the price is higher.

Another system from the same family is called value averaging. This involves buying or selling shares so that your investment increases by the same amount consistently. Take, for example, the scenario portrayed in the book *Value Averaging* (2d rev. ed., Chicago, IL: International Publishing Corporation, 1993) by former Harvard University professor of finance Michael Edleson. In January, you buy $100 worth of your chosen fund at a share price of $4.64, to get 21.55 shares. In February, the share price drops to $4.38. To increase your holdings' value by $100, you must own a total of 45.66 shares, so you purchase 24.11 shares for $105.60. You continue buying shares until July, when you have 234.11 shares at $2.99, worth $700. Then in August, the share price rises to $3.60, so you sell 11.89 shares for $42.80, to end up with a total value of $800.

when we deal with our finances, not to pay ourselves first. It's my way of paying myself first. I started with $50, and when my cash flow improved I went to $100 a month. I try not to touch it by thinking of what I'm saving for. If you know you are saving for something, it helps you to maintain the discipline of saving. A portion of your savings should be a cushion in case of an emergency and another portion should be set aside for fun, such as travel," she says.

INVESTING ADVICE: KEEP TRACK
OF YOUR FUNDS

Bridgforth recommends that African-Americans track and analyze what they're doing with their money. "Don't focus on being consumers but rather on becoming owners and entrepreneurs," she says. "It takes three minutes a day to write down where you spent your money in a day and then total that on a weekly basis. If you are tracking daily and totaling weekly, you're able to gauge your money. The important thing is to develop a plan and track it and analyze it."

Bridgforth has an unconventional way of looking at excess cash. If someone inherited $50,000, he or she should "look at their current situation and see what areas have gone unmet for a period of time. This may be contributing to a sense of scarcity or lack. You also may want to pay off debt with some of those funds, and it's also important that some of the money gets saved or invested. But, more importantly, you have to deal with your sense of deprivation first and then move from there to looking at debt. If there are some things you need, like decent underwear, go out and buy some. The money doesn't have to be put all in one area. But, make sure that 50% of it is invested in savings or real estate."

THE LAST WORD

BRIDGFORTH WANTS AFRICAN-AMERICANS TO take a holistic approach to money management. "It entails first looking at the emotional aspects of your relationship to money. What are your belief systems with respect to money? What are your attitudes and values? These were formed in childhood, so you have to take a step back in order to get a clear sense of why it is that you are doing what you are doing as an adult. The second thing is practical, which means doing the monthly spending plan, balancing your checkbook, and not creating excessive debt. The third area is spiritual practice, utilizing meditations, affirmations, and visualizations. You have to be able to see yourself having an abundant life. Make sure you believe you deserve prosperity, that you have a prosperity consciousness instead of a poverty consciousness," she says. "To do that, it's important to identify what you learned emotionally about money when you were growing up. Put it down on paper by taking an emotional money inventory."

Chapter 8

Luther Gatling is president and CEO of Budget & Credit Counseling Services, Inc. He received his B.A. from Temple University. He currently resides in Teaneck, New Jersey, with his wife and three children.

LUTHER GATLING

LUTHER GATLING RAN A COMMUNITY CREDIT counseling center, and today he is president of the largest independent financial counseling service in the country, the only black-owned credit counseling service in America. The Budget & Credit Counseling Services (BUCCS), a nonprofit organization serving Manhattan, Queens, Brooklyn, and Long Island, New York, handles $60 million in consumer debt and sees 25,000 people per year. "It's been a tremendous success to go from the four volunteers that I started with to a staff of 100 employees," he says.

Gatling is also a credit expert for a local New York morning TV show and hosts a radio program. He was a member of the Federal Reserve Consumer Advisory Board dealing with consumer issues from 1980 to 1983.

Gatling built BUCCS from the ground up, starting in 1976 when he was working with the Community Service Society of New York (CSS) as a consumer advocate and legislative lobbyist in Albany for consumer issues. "The mission of BUCCS was to fight rising interest charges as they related to the average working person. I had tremendous concern that such a move would have the same effect on African-Americans as redlining on loans and homes. I saw it as one more attempt to keep us out of the mainstream of lending. We, as black people, historically did a lot of business with finance companies where we were charged exorbitant rates of interest, and lending institutions, at that time, were trying to compete with those finance companies that have become nonbank banks," he says. "Finance companies were allowed to charge 30% interest in New York State, and lending institutions were trying to do the same thing. So I worked hard to stop this. I put BUCCS together as an experiment just to fight those issues. When the fight was won the question was whether to continue. The demand for the service that we offered dictated that it was impossible to stop."

In addition to lobbying the state legislature, Gatling's BUCCS was also helping deserted, divorced, and battered women deal with their finances. Gatling had four volunteers and rent-free office space at the CSS headquarters until the state legislature squashed the idea of raising the interest that lending institutions could charge. Gatling worked out of CSS's office space for a time while BUCCS was becoming incorporated as a separate entity. Gatling has had to move to larger offices several times. He's contemplating opening more offices in the Bronx, Harlem, and New Jersey because of demand.

"When I spun it out, I had to find money and office space. It was a nonprofit organization and it was difficult to get financing. It became a mission, because the people we were helping were in such a need, and no one else was serving them. I borrowed money against my home, mortgaged my house, and took no salary. I paid rent out of my own money while trying to raise funds from philanthropic foundations. The first grant was from the New York Foundation, and then came a small grant from the United Way. I brought in volunteers, people who weren't paid," he says. "It wasn't easy. My wife worked and supported us until it started catching on and little by little I was able to eke out a salary."

BUCCS survived on contributions until 1985, when the organization got a state license for debt pooling (a legal term for credit counseling), which enabled Gatling to charge fees for its services and get grants from the creditor community.

FINANCIAL ADVICE: START SOLVING YOUR CREDIT PROBLEMS

"The first thing we do is come up with a budget. You sit down with a counselor and put your lifestyle on a piece of paper. We look at your cash flow—how much you take home and where it goes. We look at the basic things like rent, electricity, gas, and entertainment. Then we take a look at what should be left over from your living expenses, and we look at how much debt you're in. We divide whatever surplus there is in your budget into whatever debt you owe and determine how much time it will take you to get out of debt. In most cases, you have to go back and work on the budget. We set up a way so you can get out of debt with dignity. The next thing we do is contact each one of your creditors. In some cases we are able to get finance and interest charges waived. We consolidate your debt into one monthly payment that you can afford to pay back. Our ratio of success is very high. Something like 85% of the people who come to us follow through and get their debts repaid," he says. "It's not our feeling that people should not have credit. We're trying to get people out of trouble and back into the credit system."

Although Gatling set out to serve the black community, he says credit counseling crosses all lines. "People we see now reach every ethnic group that there is. You name it, they are clients of ours. We counsel people with salaries ranging from $10,000 to $500,000. Credit problems don't just reach the poor—they reach every facet of our society," he says.

Gatling says that BUCCS is the only credit counseling center in America that helps people with bankruptcy. "Seven percent of the people we see end up in bankruptcy because their problems are so far gone that there isn't another way. When that happens, we help them with that. We have two lawyers on staff and we do the bankruptcies for people right here. The idea is to rehabilitate them so that even persons who went that far can get a fresh start. It's a last resort. What we like to do is handle people before they get in a jam to show them how to deal with credit. Unfortunately, we're like a doctor. People only come to the doctor when they hurt," he says. "About 4% of people come in just for budgeting, and 96% come in for credit problems."

The difference between BUCCS and other credit counseling centers around the country, aside from being African-American–owned, is that the board of directors of BUCCS are not from the lending institutions. "In other counseling services, creditors sit on their boards. BUCCS is the largest independent counseling center. If you have creditors on your board, their vested interest will be in collecting money for the company they work for. We will never have creditors on our board. Our board of directors is made up of people who are consumer advocates. So, we can protect the interests of the consumer," he says.

In his opinion, African-Americans need to make money matters a family affair. "Many of us black men are macho. We let our family believe that we are doing better than we really are. African-American families don't talk about money to their kids. They teach them that everything is wonderful. The biggest problem we have is that we don't sit down with family and talk about finances. I've seen African-Americans who've gotten into financial trouble and not discuss it with their families until they are bankrupt or the car is repossessed. The first sign of trouble the family may see is when someone's pay is garnished," he says.

Gatling advocates talking to children about money. "The sooner you educate children about finances, the better off they'll be," he says.

One of Gatling's secrets is to pay himself 20% of his income first. "I practice what I preach. If you're making $100 a week, and you put $20 away each time, you'd be surprised how that becomes habitual," he says. "I was able to purchase a home as a result of doing that. I still pay myself first even though my income has changed dramatically since those years. Now I invest in various instruments." He will only say that he's invested in mutual funds and has a 401(k) account.

Gatling, who is president of One Hundred Black Men, a service organization, says that one way to ensure that you save 20% each paycheck is by having the money deducted automatically. "I'd love to see all African-Americans save 20% of their income to start. It's hard, but it can be done. You have to involve the family. My wife is very involved in what we do financially," he says. "Taking a payroll deduction that goes directly into savings is a great way to start. Be realistic. Don't do it so that you can't survive. Sit down and figure out your lifestyle. Figure out how much you can comfortably give yourself. Get the family into the habit. If your children can see that this is what mom and dad are doing, they'll do the same thing. They pick it up from you."

Gatling says it's important to save because you never know when an investment opportunity will come your way. It's best to be prepared. "You've got to pay to play," he says.

Gatling says, "One of the biggest problems is understanding the credit system. How does it work? How should you get loans? What are interest charges all about?

Another thing we do too often is we co-sign for relatives without understanding that when you co-sign you're not giving a character reference; you're saying that you are liable for the debt. When you co-sign, you're 100% liable; you're a co-owner of that bill."

He recommends that everyone get a copy of his or her credit report. "It's a report card, and you want to know what your rating is. Get it once a year, because there are few functions in your lifetime when your credit report doesn't come into play. It can affect whether you get a job or rent an apartment. It determines whether you play the game or not," Gatling says.

If you already have bad credit, Gatling says the first step is recognizing that you are in financial trouble. "When you are only paying minimum monthly payments, you are in trouble. Contact every one of your creditors so that you can pay them back, or a counseling service will do all that for you. One of the biggest services we offer here is we contact creditors and make the deal, because negotiating with creditors is difficult. They can be really tough. We do the negotiations for the person," he says.

Gatling says the belief that bad credit will be erased in seven years is a myth. "It can stay on your credit report for 21 years, because if you haven't paid it in seven years, they just update the file, which can be done three consecutive times. The bottom line is you can run but you can't hide. It's just not true that your credit will be erased in seven years. You've got to figure how you can get this debt paid off. Some people will run to these places that will get you a new Social Security number. But that goes on your report too, and creditors see that something fishy is going on. Two Social Security numbers is a red alert to creditors.

People who try to hide are only fooling themselves," he says.

But, Gatling warns against consulting with credit repair agencies who say they can repair your credit for a $1,500 fee. "The way people can repair their credit once they've gotten back on the straight and narrow is by establishing some good history on their credit reports. I call it the Gatlin Mechanism. Start saving money in a bank account, and once you've reached $1,500 go to the bank and say you want to borrow a thousand dollars. They will loan it to you because it's collateralized. Never leave the bank with the money. Once you get the loan, put it into a savings account. Now you've got $2,500, which pays you interest. For a six-month period of time, pay the loan back out of the money in the savings account every month. Then put it on your credit report as positive information. It works," he says. "The other way is to get a collateralized credit card. You put up a certain amount of money, and you'll get the card because you've collateralized it. The secret is to make sure the bank you collateralized with actually puts your money into a CD account for you. That will be part of the agreement. After you handle the card properly for two years the bank will then offer you an uncollateralized card and give you your money back plus the interest it gained in the CD."

Another piece of advice from Gatling: Don't be duped by credit card companies that offer 5.9% interest. First, get out your magnifying glass. "Some of them carry kickers on them where the first three months they'll offer you a low rate of interest and then later on down the line, the rate is kicked up to 19% or 20% interest," he says. "There are other gimmicks when you transfer money from one card to another. The first money that's transferred gets that

5.9% interest and any new purchases go up in interest. So, you have to read the fine print. We're so eager to just get the credit that we don't look the gift horse in the mouth. You have to count and make sure that all 32 teeth are there. Remember there are people out there all the time trying to get your money from you, and that's a profession."

Gatling says one way to help avoid credit trouble is to have no more than three credit cards. The cards in his own billfold include a revolving credit card, a charge card, and a debit card. "We try to amass credit cards, and that's a huge mistake. What people don't realize is that if they amass these cards, then when they try to do something major, they are rejected. The average American (including African-Americans) carries a dozen credit cards. If creditors see you have all these cards, you're turned down because you have too much credit available to you," he says.

Instead, Gatling advises that African-Americans be more conscious of the fact that they live in a capitalistic society. "There's nothing wrong with credit. Just use it as leverage. You have to take care of it, and that means monitoring and minding it. No matter how much it is, you have to control it. You don't have to keep up with the Joneses. The only Jones you have to keep up with is yourself, because what you're looking for is freedom. The goal should be to have financial independence where you control your own destiny. You've got to find innovative ways so that you don't become a slave to the system. You have to dictate how the system works for you. You have to be in control rather than having someone else in control," he says.

With $50 a month, Gatling says he'd prefer to see people save instead of invest. "There isn't a lot you can do in terms of investing with $50. Some people would say that there is, but I would put it somewhere safe—a bank or credit union. Watch it grow, and when it gets to a certain point then look at what other vehicles are open. The first plan is to save; that's a major step right there. You'll be so many light-years ahead of everybody else," he says.

THE LAST WORD

BEFORE INVESTING A $50,000 WINDFALL, GATLING says it's important to find a trustworthy financial planner who can invest the money for you. He suggests polling friends and family for recommendations. "Put the money someplace safe. Then, take the time and pains to interview people who are financial planners. Make sure that they give you a list of people they have done business for. Go and talk to those people. You have to do this because there are thieves, crooks, and con people out there. The best con people in the world are the smoothest. Don't buy investments over the telephone. Search out these financial professionals because the life you're saving is your own," he says.

Part IV

GOVERNMENT

Chapter 9

Isaac Hunt, Jr., is a commissioner of the Securities and Exchange Commission. He received his L.L.B. from the University of Virginia School of Law and B.A. from Fisk University. He currently resides in Washington, D.C.

COURTESY OF ISAAC HUNT, JR., © ANKERS IMAGING

ISAAC HUNT, JR.

ISAAC HUNT, JR., IS ONE OF THE FIVE SEC COMMISsioners in the nation's capital, and to prove it, Hunt wears SEC-engraved cufflinks, which he ordered with SEC chairman Arthur Levitt.

The SEC enforces federal securities laws, which basically consist of six statutes enacted between 1933 and 1940, and periodically amended in the intervening years, and one enacted in 1970. They are: Securities Act of 1933, Securities Exchange Act of 1934, Public Utility Holding Company Act of 1935, Trust Indenture Act of 1939, Investment Company Act of 1940, Investment Advisors Act of 1940, and the Securities Investor Protection Act of 1970.

"The SEC regulates the public offering of securities in America and also regulates the operations of the securities exchanges, the markets. It regulates essentially those companies that sell securities to the market," Hunt says. "I do the same thing that the other commissioners do. We adjudicate cases, because we are a law enforcement agency. Our staff brings cases to us of wrongdoing in the market and we hear those cases and impose punishments on those people. We regulate the exchanges. We have oversight over securities markets. We have oversight over setting accounting standards to be used by public companies in America."

Hunt is the second African-American to serve as an SEC commissioner. He was appointed by President Clinton, confirmed by the Senate in February 1996, and will serve until June 5, 2000. Hunt says he was connected from the days that he worked on the staff of the SEC. "The White House learned about me through Chairman Levitt, who learned about me through these people who are in the securities business, who've been friends for a long time," he says.

In 1962, the commissioner was the second African-American to graduate from the University of Virginia Law School. He was only the second black lawyer to serve on the staff of the SEC (from 1962 to 1967). Finally, he was the first African-American to serve in the general counsel's office of the Department of the Army (from 1979 to 1981).

"My first job out of law school was here at the commission as a staff attorney, and then I taught securities law for many years. I was a professor at Catholic University School of Law in Washington, DC, and then dean of two law schools, including the former Antioch School of Law in Washington, DC, and the University of Akron in Ohio. I also practiced for a while with a firm here in Washington where we did some securities law," he says.

As a commissioner, Hunt travels around the country conducting town hall meetings for the individual investor. "We try to educate people about what they should be doing about investments. One thing we tell them is to know the investment adviser they are using—to read any information about the investments they are thinking about making carefully and consult with their investment adviser before making an investment," he says. "I think it's very important that all Americans save and put some money into various investment instruments in conventional CDs and perhaps some mutual funds. If they are going to do something speculative, they should be aware of the risk by reading and talking to people. They shouldn't put any more money in a speculative investment than they can afford to lose. No one should have all their money in various speculative investments."

Hunt says you should beware of derivatives, new companies, and cold calls from brokers. "Unless you know the people in the company, I'd stay away from investing in new companies. And, when cold-calling brokers recommend stocks that you've never heard of, I would caution against that. The bottom line is—know your investment adviser, read investment material, and if you don't know the investment adviser, get references that this person is honest and will be able to help you," he says.

The commissioner warns investors about pyramid scams. "Over the years, I have known of African-Americans who got involved in pyramid schemes. Pyramid shemes and Ponzi schemes take place around the world. It's not just a problem here in America. The Albanian government just fell because of a Ponzi scheme there," he says. In a Ponzi scheme, the people who run the scheme promise you a certain return on your money. They pay you off from the money they get from subsequent investors rather than investing the money. "It eventually collapses," says Hunt.

In addition to his domestic lectures, Hunt also travels internationally giving speeches. He's been to Russia, Greece, Italy, England, Canada, Mexico, Venezuela, and South Africa. "I've been concentrating on our international activities. We have a lot of cooperation from other securities regulators from around the world. We help other countries as they try to improve their capital markets' formation. I also do a lot of work with state regulators because each state has its own securities regulation agency," he says. "Sometimes I'm dealing with the international organization of securities regulators, worldwide organizations like ours. I go to conferences to give speeches, and I inform companies that want to raise money in our markets. I tell them what they have to do to qualify to register with us and our securities markets."

PERSONAL PORTFOLIO

Hunt spoke very briefly on the contents of his personal portfolio, preferring to talk about his work on the SEC. "I've got some stocks that I inherited from my parents. I've got some certificates of deposit, which I'm transferring into mutual funds. I'm going to vary the types of mutual funds in which I invest," he says. "I had to save for my son's college education, and now that he's finished, I'll invest more for growth rather than stability and conservation of principal, which I was doing when he was in college." He proposes doing this by picking mutual funds very carefully. "I don't think I'm going to go into any speculative investments. I'm going to invest in mutual funds from very reputable companies," he says.

Hunt adheres to a rather stringent savings plan. "I try to save about 15% to 20% of my income on an annual basis, and I'm going to try to invest most of that, diversifying my investments with mutual funds," he says.

INVESTING ADVICE: DO YOUR HOMEWORK

Commissioner Hunt is a strong advocate of doing your homework before putting down some cash. "With a mutual fund prospectus, look for the investment policy and objective of the fund, and how successful the fund has been over a period of years. As for the prospectus of an individual company, try to understand the company's prospects and its financial statement. Look at the history and experience of the management of the company, all of which would be in the prospectus, and also management's discussion and analysis of what it sees for the company in the future," he says.

The commissioner feels strongly about recruiting more African-Americans into the financial services industry by exposing minority students to the world of finance. "It's an exciting and interesting business to be engaged in. You can help people to make sound investments and you can earn yourself a decent income," he says.

In addition to using his position to recruit more

African-Americans into the finance industry, Hunt has also spoken out on some political issues in recent years. He was a critic of former President George Bush's decision to nominate Clarence Thomas to the Supreme Court. He also criticized President Clinton's withdrawal of the 1993 nomination of Lani Guinier as the Justice Department's civil rights chief. He is currently a strong advocate for affirmative action.

THE LAST WORD

WHEN ASKED WHAT AFRICAN-AMERICANS CAN do to control their financial futures, Hunt has this to say: "Spend money wisely and invest wisely. For all of us, we shouldn't overextend ourselves in terms of debt. We should live within our means and should try to save and invest some money wisely. People can't achieve high finance on a low budget. Nobody can do that. Obviously, the most unfortunate among us are struggling to make ends meet, but for those of us who have some money that we don't have to spend on day-to-day needs, I think we ought to try to save some of it and invest it for the future."

He believes that there is no excuse for African-Americans not to know about investing. "There are lots of books, TV programs, magazines, and special news networks with a lot of information about finances, money, and investing," he says.

Part V

MONEY/
INVESTMENT
MANAGEMENT

Chapter 10

Barbara Bowles is president and CEO of The Kenwood Group, Inc. She received her B.A. from Fisk University and M.B.A. from the University of Chicago. She currently resides in Chicago, Illinois, with her husband and son.

BARBARA BOWLES

THE KENWOOD GROUP, OWNED AND OPERATED BY Barbara Bowles, was the first African-American female-owned firm to launch a mutual fund, called the Kenwood Growth and Income Fund.

The Kenwood Group has about $300 million in assets under management and a total of 18 institutional clients. About half of the client list are public companies, 40% are privately-held corporations, and 10% are endowment funds. Some clients include the City of Atlanta, the District of Columbia Retirement Board, Quaker Oats Company, Woolworth Corporation, and the Field Museum of Natural History in Chicago.

The minimum investment is $1 million, and the money must be tax-exempt, which rules out the retail end of investments. Individual investors are served through the mutual fund.

Prior to starting the Chicago-based Kenwood Group, Bowles served as corporate vice president for Kraft, heading the investor relations department. From 1981 to 1984, she was assistant vice president and director of investor relations for Beatrice Companies. She got most of her banking experience as vice president for trust investments for the First National Bank of Chicago, where she worked for 13 years.

She started the Kenwood Group eight years ago. "I left Kraft as vice president of investor relations after the company was acquired by Philip Morris. I decided to do something that I'd always wanted to do, which was to start a money management business. The problem with starting a money management business when you've been in corporate America is that you have no track record. You have no one to just rush out and give you money to invest. So, I had to rely on word of mouth and networking to get a client. We were very fortunate six months after we were in business to get our first client," she says. "Quaker Oats was my first client. I got to know them in the food business, which was my business before I started the investment firm. Relationships are important. How successful you are in other modes of life can help you become successful in this business."

To open the Kenwood Group, Bowles took the severance pay she received from Kraft to open an office in June 1989. "Then we started knocking on doors, literally. I initially had a partner for about a year. It took three years to break even. I spent about $250,000 of my own money. The reason it took that much money is because it takes a long time to get business. The first couple of pieces of business I got didn't allow me to make any money. So, you are still financing the business while you are trying to grow into earning enough money to support the business," she says.

Bowles was fortunate; she had a working husband. "I also had some money saved. The money I had left over from my previous job and my savings plus my husband working every day helped support us during that time. I was lucky, too, because the first people I hired knew that they'd have to sacrifice a little bit in terms of their salary to help support the business until it became profitable, and some of those people today are some of my most loyal employees," she says.

PERSONAL PORTFOLIO

Bowles estimates that her net worth today is over $1 million, and she attributes that to having started her own business. "In my family we are comfortable and our business is profitable, but it didn't get that way overnight. We have been managing money profitably now for the past three years, and this is a very lucrative business. It's a high-margin business. In addition, it's easier to amass a large net income if you own your business rather than working in corporate America. I didn't expect to become wealthy working in corporate America. I have had the opportunity to become wealthy by starting my own company. The worth of the business has gone up and a large part of my net worth is tied into the business. I'm not only living off an income but I'm living off a growing income in a growing business that I own. So I have two ways of growing my fortune," she says.

One of her secrets to amassing a large personal fortune is that she takes very little salary from her company's profits. "What I take out of my company is what I need to maintain my lifestyle. The rest of the money stays in the company. My husband has extra income, and the money we have left over we put in the bond market and stock market. I consider that the best form of saving. I don't go out and buy a new car every time I get extra money. I don't spend a lot of money on material things. We have a nice house and two cars, but that's enough. I don't need to keep adding things to my life to make me feel better. I advocate 'Buy what you need and the rest invest,' " she says.

Most of Bowles's excess cash is invested in the market and she says she has very little money in the bank. "I have a 401(k) plan that's about 50–50 in equities and bonds. I have a savings plan that's 50–50 in equities and bonds, and I have all of my profit sharing money tied up in my company and in the stock market. I think that's the best opportunity for me to grow my wealth. If I had extra dollars, I'd put it in my firm, because I think my company will grow faster the more money I reinvest in it. Each year that we make money, we just plow it back into the business," she says.

Bowles, in her personal investing life, invests in a basket of stocks and bonds. "I tend to be a little bit more aggressive in my own personal style simply because I have a lot of money in the bond market. So, having money in fixed-income securities mitigates the risk I'm taking in the stock market personally," she says. "I have about 50% in bonds and 50% in stocks, and obviously in the last four years that's been a mistake. All the money should have been in the stock market. I tend to be an aggressive equity investor and so consequently I have a larger asset mix in bonds."

She also invests in her own mutual fund, because she's says it's easier for her to put her money there than to think about what stocks to buy. "It would be difficult for me to buy any of those individual stocks because I would run into SEC rules. So, the best way for me to buy stocks that I like is to buy my mutual fund," she says.

Bowles says that African-Americans should look beyond banks and invest in the stock market for the long term in order to reduce risk. "There are other avenues of performance, like equities and bonds. Although people have become very familiar with the securities market, minorities are still not investing at high levels. They are still investing at very low levels. If I had a lot of money, the first thing I'd do is put it away and not spend it. The second thing I'd do is determine where I'd want to invest it. My first choice would be the stock market, because it has a history of longer-term success. The real key is longer-term investments rather than short-term investments," she says. "A lot of people don't want to invest in the stock market because they think they're taking significant risk. But risk is only relevant in the market over short periods of time.

Time eliminates risk. If you are willing to invest for more than three or four years, you've eliminated most of the risk of the market, and a lot of people don't realize that."

Bowles is keen on investing in mutual funds. "It's probably the best way because it allows you to get a diversified portfolio without figuring out what individual stocks to invest in. Make sure that you're investing in companies that you believe in. Our particular mode of investing is mid-cap value, meaning we do not buy very large companies. We buy medium-cap companies and we're value-oriented, which means that we're buying companies that have assets worth more than what the stock is selling for or companies that have good growth profiles but have had some difficulty and their stock price has come down. Basically, we like companies that very few people are following. They tend to be inefficiently priced when that is the case," she says.

Bowles calls herself a value investor, which entails buying companies that no one else wants and consequently buying low and selling high. "We have a contrarian bent in our process. We like to buy companies that sell at a lower value than the market puts on itself. We buy companies that sell at low P/E [price/earnings] ratios. We like companies where the market value is low in relationship to the book value. My investing techniques personally are the same as my investing techniques for my company. Individuals have a natural style, even us institutional investors," she says.

Bowles is the actual fund manager, but she also has three portfolio managers/analysts who help her make decisions. The Kenwood Growth and Income Fund, which has about $2 million in assets, is a diversified portfolio containing between 40 and 50 stocks. Bowles says she reaps benefits from 30 to 40 of these stocks at a time. When the stocks reach their fair value targets, Bowles sells them. "The most exciting investment since I've been in business was owning Citicorp. We bought it when it was considered a possible takeover target, and people thought it could go bankrupt in the late 1980s and early 1990s. The stock got down to $10 a share and today it's trading at $130. We sold it at $100, and that's a tenfold investment performance, which is extremely rare in our business even over a five-year period of time," she says.

INVESTING ADVICE: STOCKS AND BONDS AND INVEST IN YOUR EMPLOYER

Aside from investing 50% in stocks and bonds, Bowles recommends stashing money short-term for a rainy day in a money market account. Another of her secrets is to invest in the company that you work for as long as you don't invest all of your money in the one stock. Some of the best-performing stocks that Bowles owns she inherited from her previous positions at Philip Morris and the First National Bank of Chicago. "First National Bank of Chicago recently merged with the National Bank of Detroit, and both of those stocks have done extremely well. My cost on First National Bank of Chicago stock was $7 15 years ago, and it has gone up to $65 a share. Philip Morris stock I bought at $10 in 1989, and the stock is at $45," she says. "Philip Morris had a stock purchase plan, and my choice was not only to buy it but to keep the stock after I left the company. So often, we make the mistake of selling the stock after leaving the company."

Before investing, though, Bowles advises people to educate themselves about investing. "If you choose to get educated, it takes time. We recommend that you read a business periodical every day because you have to understand the jargon. Know what a P/E ratio means. Know what market-to-book ratio means. You have to understand a company's long-term growth rate and its growth strategy and then determine how it sells in relation to its industry group. It's not all that easy to get at all of those issues," she says.

Bowles recommends an asset allocation for people in the 40- to 70-years-old group. She advises having 60% to 70% of assets in equities, presuming they have no need for the money in three to four years. About 25% to 35% should be in bonds and 5% in cash. "In order to be appropriately diversified you probably need $10,000, but you can do it with a mutual fund for a couple of thousand dollars," she says.

With a $50,000 inheritance, Bowles says she'd put 60% in the stock market and 35% in the bond market, and keep 5% in cash. "Right now, the conservative place to put your money is in financial institutions. They are still

---

INVESTING BASICS

P/E ratio (price/earnings ratio) is what a company's stock is selling at in relation to its earnings. For example, if Philip Morris has a P/E of 20, that means that the stock sells at 20 times the earnings per share (EPS).

Earnings per share (EPS) is earnings or net income divided by the number of shares outstanding.

Market-to-book ratio is the market value of a company divided by net assets.

Market value of a company is the number of shares outstanding times the stock price.

fairly cheap. Utilities have a lot of growth opportunity. They are very cheap because of the deregulated environment and the transition that's going on there. I would consider some consumer companies, such as food and service-oriented companies, whose P/E ratios are lower than the market," she says.

With $50 a month to invest, Bowles recommends investing in a mutual fund. "Our mutual fund will take you if you are willing to put in $100 a month, but some will accept $50 a month. You have to look harder for that. There's another way to do it: If you have only $50 a month, you could put in money every two months. Our firm says we want a $100-a-month investor, but if you call us up and tell us that you're committed to doing a $100 a month every other month, we'll probably accept you," she says.

Bowles says investors should be aware that the market can go down. "You have to be a very cautious investor all the time. You can't rely on history to determine what the future is in this business. Now that the market has gone up so much over the past 10 years, people think that it will never go down. Be wary of that and be wary of the interest rate environment. If interest rates go up, both stock and bonds could be hurt. People have to be aware of the economic environment that they live in. They don't have to be sophisticated, but they have to listen to the news and see what's going on," she says. "Keep in mind that any outside, external surprise can affect the market. For instance, the Lockerbie bombing and energy crisis affected the market. People must be patient investors and realize that though the market goes up and down over time, it will more than likely go back up. You shouldn't take your money out of the market at the first sign of a big drop."

THE LAST WORD

THE MOST IMPORTANT THING THAT AFRICAN-Americans need to do with their money, Bowles says, is to quit spending it on material possessions and instead invest it in ways that will help them increase their net worth. "Buy the house rather than rent. Don't just put your money in the bank unless that's the only place you can think of. But put it there rather than spend it. You can earn more money buying Treasury bills than you can in the cash markets," she says. "Our biggest problem is that we're not educated enough to realize that you have to have money to grow money. If we work hard we can live comfortably, but nine times out of ten we will not be able to grow our net worth. Working and earning an income does not, in and of itself, grow net worth. Always put some money aside and invest that money."

Bowles says that in addition to setting aside money at the end of each day, African-Americans need to leave money behind for their children so that they can have a head start in accumulating wealth and controlling their financial futures. "One of the reasons that young white people are so successful is because their parents have left them an inheritance, which does a lot for your ego. We usually have nothing. We're always starting from scratch and therefore we can never really get ahead. The idea is to leave something behind so that our children won't have to scrape as much as we did. We're learning how to do that. African-Americans are becoming smarter, more astute, and more sophisticated about investing," she says.

Chapter 11

Eddie Brown is president of Brown Capital Management. He received his B.A. from Howard University, M.S. from New York University, and M.B.A. from the Indiana School of Business. He currently resides in Glen Arm, Maryland, with his wife and two children.

EDDIE BROWN

EDDIE BROWN STARTED THE SECOND AFRICAN-American–owned money management firm in the United States a few short months after John Rogers started Ariel Capital Management. Brown Capital Management was established in Baltimore, Maryland, in July 1983 after Brown had worked for T. Rowe Price, an investment management firm, for 10 years as a portfolio manager and vice president. He managed major institutional clients such as pension and endowment funds.

Brown, 56, was the first African-American money manager hired by T. Rowe Price, in 1973. In May 1979, he became the first African-American panelist on *Wall Street Week*. "Even from a young age, I always had this entrepreneurial drive or spirit. I was in my early forties and figured if I was ever going to do something entrepreneurial I should get moving, because there's always a chance of failure—which I had no idea of doing, but you want to give it a try at an age when you'll still have time to recover if you fail," he says.

Brown is very fond of doing his homework. Before founding his business, he did a study of new, small businesses to see what he needed to do to be successful. He found that two of the pitfalls of starting a small business were undercapitalization and starting with fancy offices and a lot of overhead costs.

Because he didn't want to take any business from T. Rowe Price, Brown started his firm with no clients, assets, or income. In other words, he started his business from scratch. Brown says he's never made a cold call. To get clients, Brown contacted CPAs, trust and estate attorneys, and small pension plan administrators, because they worked with plans that could be prospective clients. "I networked with them, letting them know I existed, and encouraged them to refer people to Brown Capital Management. I was color-blind in terms of networking. Very few of my early clients were black. I got the largest support in the early days from the Jewish community," he says.

Brown prospered. Coincidentally, the day he set up shop in the study of his home, a letter arrived from a woman in Washington, DC, who had just received money from a medical malpractice settlement. She became Brown's first client, and within a month Brown had office space and an administrative assistant.

"I had quite a bit of T. Rowe Price stock, which gave me some independence, and I had sufficient personal financial assets to be able to survive without taking a salary and to fund the business from an operational standpoint for up to three years," he says.

Brown Capital Management has $3.1 billion under management, most of it institutional money. The largest clients include California Public Employees Retirement System (CALPERS), the state of Oregon Retirement System, the Calvert Group, the California State Teacher's Retirement System (CALSTRS), and the state of Connecticut Retirement System. Today, Brown's minimum investment requirement is $5 million, up from $100,000 when the firm first started 14 years ago.

In addition to managing institutional money, Brown also founded three mutual funds in August 1992. They are the $6.4 million Brown Capital Equity Fund, the $5.4 million Brown Capital Balanced Fund, and the $9.4 million Brown Capital Small Company Fund. As president of Brown Capital Management, Brown acts as a portfolio manager and analyst, researching companies.

"Among the three funds, the balanced fund is most conservative, the equity fund is considered moderate-risk, and the small company fund is the most aggressive. We've tried to structure a series of funds that would hit different risk tolerances, from conservative to moderate to aggressive," he says.

The most important investments that Brown is still reaping benefits from are his stake in T. Rowe Price stock and his investment in Brown Capital Management. He owns 100% of Brown Capital Management stock. But Brown declined to disclose how much his company is worth and how much his stock in T. Rowe Price is worth.

"In 1986, T. Rowe Price went public, and now it's publicly traded. About five or six years ago my holding of the stock was the single most important asset in my personal balance sheet. I'm glad I held onto the stock. Today the equity of Brown Capital Management is by far our largest single asset. The value of that is many times greater than the value of T. Rowe Price stock," he says. "The most important was building Brown Capital Management. My second largest asset is T. Rowe Price stock."

PERSONAL PORTFOLIO

Unlike other finance experts interviewed, Brown wouldn't disclose what individual stocks he's invested in. He would say only that he owns several investment properties, including the building where his office is located. He is also invested in his companies' mutual funds. Some larger holdings of Brown's mutual funds include T. Rowe Price Associates, Cardinal Health, Home Depot, and Cisco Systems.

Brown refused to discuss his personal fortune, but it's enough to know that he owns 100% of his company. He says his secret is practicing personally the same investment discipline that he practices for his clients. He doesn't buy every single stock that he buys for clients, but he generally follows his company's investing guidelines.

Brown doesn't have a savings account. Instead, he invests whatever cash is left over from his monthly budget. "We have a budget that is fairly modest. I haven't changed my lifestyle as my income has grown over the years. We still live in the same house that we've lived in for 20 years. It's different since the income is much greater than the budgeted needs, which means that there is a lot of excess cash that's many times our budgeted expenses. I invest that on a regular basis. That's what I consider saving," he says.

Brown calls himself a "garp" investor, which is growth at a reasonable price, as opposed to "gap," which is growth at any price. "We seek to pay less than the market in terms of price-to-earnings ratio for superior companies. We measure superior companies in several ways, besides well managed companies. We want profitability as measured by return on equity much greater than the stock market and prospective earnings per share growth of the companies much greater than the overall market, which varies with market conditions," he says. "Our investment time horizon when we are making assessments of the prospects of a company in terms of their revenue growth and prospective earnings per share growth is the next three to five years."

Brown also considers the interest rate environment when selecting stock. "In low interest rate environments we're willing to pay a premium for growth whereas in higher interest rate environments we're willing to pay a discount for growth. How much we're willing to pay with respect to P/E to growth is not a fixed ratio. But, it varies according to the interest rate environment," he says.

In order to get investing ideas, Brown reads many of

the major financial publications, such as *Fortune* and *Forbes*. He also observes trends in the marketplace as a consumer and attends investment conferences sponsored by Wall Street firms, such as William Blair, Montgomery Securities, and Alex. Brown.

"At these conferences they bring in top managements of various companies, so we get a chance to see and hear the stories on the companies directly. Also, we're covered by several of the major Wall Street firms and have several analysts come into our offices to talk about investment ideas. As we've grown, we're getting visits from top managements of companies to talk about their companies and have us ask questions. So, there are many sources," he says.

INVESTING ADVICE: OVERSEAS FUNDS

Brown recommends investing in international mutual funds, because there are so many places outside the country that are growing faster economically than the United States. "It'd be wise to have 10% to 15% of one's investable assets in an international stock mutual fund. Having a combination of domestic and international investments makes sense," he says.

To reduce risk in the stock market, Brown advises doing your homework on a company. "We know the companies that we invest in very well. We visit smaller companies at their locations. For the mid- to larger-sized companies, we talk with management by telephone and we see most of them at investment conferences, and in many cases we have smaller group meetings with them at these conferences," he says.

Brown says that investing is not something that African-Americans as a race have been aware of. "The goal should be to seek financial independence by way of investing, which requires patience and time. With the power of compounding, you'll be surprised by the nest egg established 10 to 15 years down the road," he says.

With a $50,000 inheritance, Brown recommends investing 80% in a domestic equity mutual fund and 20% in an international stock fund. In terms of pitfalls, Brown says beware of being frightened out of the market, selling at the wrong time, and investing based on tips from friends. "You're not investing based on any knowledge, and the person who gave you the tip won't be there to tell you when to sell it. People should invest based on knowledge, and that's why it's better to use professional management, such as mutual fund managers or private money managers," he says.

THE LAST WORD

BROWN ADVISES UNDERSTANDING THE POWER OF compounding return. "Having a consistent investment program, over time, invested in common stocks or mutual funds is the best way to accumulate wealth or financial independence. You have to work at it, and you have to have a consistent plan where you are investing a portion of your check every month in good times in the market and bad times. That's dollar cost averaging," he says. "Invest as much as you can spare. The problem for younger people is they should have a budget, and part of that budget should be a certain amount for investing. Otherwise, they will never have anything available— because they tend to spend above their means."

Chapter 12

Nathaniel Carter is president and chief investment officer of Lakefront Capital Investors, Inc. He received his B.A. from Georgetown University and M.B.A. from Harvard University. He currently resides in Cleveland, Ohio, with his wife and three daughters.

NATHANIEL CARTER

WHEN NATHANIEL CARTER AND I TALKED LAST April 15, the money manager was preoccupied with Intel. Intel, the Santa Clara, California–based company, had just reported first-quarter earnings and warned the press that it expected sales to be flat to only slightly higher in the second quarter. When the company released its report, shares fell to $129.875 from $133.75.

Carter, president and chief investment officer of Lakefront Capital Investors, said he too was concerned about the performance of the stock. "It's experiencing short-term volatility, but I'm still going to own it," he said. "A lot of people will trade in and out. We tend not to do that, because it would hurt our mandate. We still like Intel for the long term."

This preoccupation with stock is just what you'd expect from someone who is managing your pension or mutual fund. As founder and owner of Lakefront, Carter does both. Five years ago, he started the first African-American–owned investment management firm in Ohio. Based in Cleveland, Lakefront manages $22 million in institutional assets. Among Lakefront's clients are the Eaton Corporation, Ohio Edison Company, and the Ohio Police and Fireman's Pension Fund. Carter says his goal is to have $100 million under management by the end of 1998.

After graduating with a BA from Georgetown University, Carter worked for three years with the Chase Manhattan Bank in New York as a credit analyst and later as a corporate lending officer. He then got an MBA from Harvard and spent two years with the investment banking firm Drexel Burnham Lambert Inc., specializing in corporate finance. In 1990, Carter decided to go home to Cleveland and start his own business.

"I felt that there would be some advantage because

the cost of doing business is lower in Ohio, and the Midwest has a more wholesome image. I just didn't feel there was an advantage for me to be in New York any longer," he says.

To start his own business, Carter aligned himself with an existing brokerage firm called Roulston & Company. He was able to use Roulston's equipment and set up an office for himself there. He registered with the SEC and got himself incorporated. He had no money, so he appealed to friends and raised about $75,000 to pay for marketing and some salary for himself. He received no other salary for the next three years. "I got an understanding of the operational aspects of the business from working within Roulston. I had worked in commercial banking and investment banking, so I had a pretty good understanding of how to analyze companies. But I had never picked a stock. This experience helped me develop an investing style. I found that I was best suited to invest in large companies that were undervalued," he says.

After working under the auspices of Roulston for a year, Carter struck out on his own. Shortly thereafter, in October 1992, he received his first account—the Ohio Police and Fireman's Pension Fund, which had $6 billion in assets, of which Carter manages $9 million.

"They were looking to hire an African-American money management firm. So, I went to Columbus to meet with board members and to try to sell myself," Carter says. "It was difficult, because I didn't have any money under management. As a result of trying to sell myself I made connections, and they hired me based on my investing style and the dummy portfolio I had put together."

Carter says he invests in large-cap companies in growth industries with market capitalizations exceeding

$1 billion that are trading at a discount to the market. "The market capitalization requirement narrows our choices down to 1,200 companies. Then, we look at those companies that are trading at or below 110% of the market P/E, and that whittles down our selection to about 600 companies," he says. "That's how we determine if it's a value stock. We also look at price-to-book and price–to–cash flow, and stocks that are trading at or below market level."

Carter applies this same investing strategy to the mutual fund he started up along with the KeyCorp fund group on March 1, 1997. Like other funds, the Victory Lakefront Fund is aimed at African-American investors. Its distinction is offering shareholder activism for the sake of corporate diversity. Carter stresses that the fund is not what is termed a "socially responsible" fund. It doesn't exclude companies; rather, the fund simply focuses on diversity once it owns shares in a company. "The premise is that African-Americans care about the return on their investment dollar, and they are concerned with what the companies are doing with respect to diversity. So we do the work for them in terms of asserting diversity initiatives," Carter says.

"Once the fund invests in a company, we'll look into what their diversity practices are and impart to them the importance of diversity initiatives. We establish who the diversity person is and ask for information on company policy. If, after the information-gathering stage, we see the company needs improvement, we'll go to the company's diversity person and try to make him or her aware of why it's important to practice diversity. We may even appeal to the chairman of the board or the president."

Carter firmly believes that African-Americans can

make a difference in corporate America with respect to diversity by becoming active shareholders in American companies, while simultaneously earning returns from their investments.

Even as individual shareholders African-Americans can make a difference by calling up the company or writing a letter asking about diversity programs at the company whose shares they own. "You don't want to be antagonistic. You're just trying to make the company aware that diversity is good from an economic standpoint," he says. "One vote means something. You can choose to vote for none of the board of directors and then call investor relations to find out why the company has no African-Americans on its board." After an individual investor finds out about a company's diversity program, the person should take action. "If you don't like their policies, then you can sell the stock and let them know why. Then, you move on to the next opportunity."

The Lakefront Victory Fund owns shares in Texaco and has been active in garnering information about the company's diversity programs. Texaco executives were allegedly taped making biased remarks about blacks in the company. As a result, the company agreed to pay $176 million to settle a discrimination case and to give plaintiffs an 11% pay raise.

"Texaco has been forthright in providing their diversity information. We sent them a letter requesting a sit-down meeting with their diversity representative, which we expect will happen. They understand that we are shareholders and that we have a right to discuss these issues," Carter says.

Carter is an advocate of African-Americans investing in equities, but he also believes that they should take the

---

FIVE THINGS TO DO AS A SHAREHOLDER ACTIVIST

1. Write a letter to the company and ask about diversity issues.
2. Call the company and speak with investor relations about the number of African-American managers on staff.
3. Organize a group of people who own shares in the same company and send a petition requesting that an African-American be appointed to the board of directors.
4. Attend the board meetings and make yourself known as an African-American shareholder.
5. Vote on company issues whenever you receive a proxy in the mail.

---

emotion out of the investment process by focusing more on performance than social responsibility.

"Everything we do doesn't have to fall into the category of having a strong social component. We need to be focused on increasing our wealth through the stock market. Once we do that and get familiar with how the market works, then we can include social responsibility. But don't give up performance for social responsibility," he says. "Be your own social engineer by becoming a shareholder activist or donating time to your community. I'm not saying not to be concerned at all, but with respect to diversity most of the companies want to do the right thing; they just need prodding."

When asked about his favorite stocks, Carter mentioned K-mart and Reebok. He bought K-mart in April 1996 for $8.50 a share. It was trading at $12.75 about one year later. "It's had some trouble over the years. It went through a management shift two years ago. It was beaten down and wasn't attractive, but we saw it as an opportunity after it cut out its dividends entirely," Carter says. "We bought into the stock with the belief that it had hit rock bottom. You know it's hit rock bottom when negative news comes out and it doesn't drop in price any further."

The same observation holds truc for Reebok, which Carter bought in April 1996 for $27. The stock was trading at $45 a year later. "The company was going through turmoil. The design of their shoes wasn't appealing, and the shoes didn't have good performance athletically compared to Nike. They weren't signing on the right people to promotc thc shoes, and rumors said their management wasn't up to snuff," Carter says. "The stock got down to the mid-20s and the negative news kept coming, but it stopped dropping in price. We realized it had been beaten down. Wc thought it was a good value opportunity and have enjoyed its appreciation since."

PERSONAL PORTFOLIO

Carter doesn't own any stock outside of his mutual fund, due to SEC regulations. As a result, his personal fortune is tied up in his business. Carter estimates Lakefront is worth about $1.1 million, the amount he's managing in the mutual fund. "We still need to build our asset base," he says. Despite some times when he's considered leaving his firm, Carter has persevered. "The prospect of working in corporate America knocked me around a bit. I don't want to experience the *60 Minutes* syndrome on Sunday evenings. When the clock is ticking on the television news show *60 Minutes*, you know it's time to go back to the salt mines of corporate America," he says. "I didn't like corporate America. It was endlessly stagnating. I worked a tremendous amount of hours and once Drexel went under, I decided I didn't want to do the corporate thing anymore. Basically, if I'm going to work hard, I might as well work hard for myself."

The single most important investment that Carter says he's still reaping benefits from is his Harvard MBA. It cost him about $50,000 and has dramatically added to his net worth by helping him with his business. "It gives me credibility," he says. "This society is not a meritocracy no matter what your race, which indicates that you need to function on many levels. It's not enough to be competent; you have to understand how things get done. Harvard helped me understand how business operates with respect to relationships and how things are accomplished."

INVESTING ADVICE: STEADY SAVING
AND INVESTING

Although Carter isn't adhering to a savings plan right now because he's still building his business, he recommends saving 50% of your free cash flow monthly. But, instead of parking it in a savings account, invest 40% of it in domestic securities, 20% in international securities, and the remainder in domestic fixed-income securities. "The same positive feelings you can get from buying a new watch you can also get from having money invested and watching it grow. But, before you start investing, pay off any credit card debt," he says.

The perfect asset allocation, Carter says, depends on your age. For a 20-year-old, he recommends having 90%

invested in the stock market and 10% in fixed-income securities. If you're 60 years old, invest 30% in blue-chip stocks and 70% in low-risk fixed-income securities, such as government securities or high-grade AAA corporate bonds. With a hypothetical $50,000 inheritance, Carter says he'd invest 70% in the stock market and stash the remainder in fixed-income securities.

In spite of Carter's enthusiasm about African-Americans investing in the stock market, he says there are some pitfalls to avoid. "The pitfalls are fly-by-night small companies that don't have much of a history," he says. Carter advises sticking with companies you know. "You can access information on Intel pretty easily, but there are other smaller high-tech companies that can be purely speculative. If you don't have an understanding of what they do, then you shouldn't be buying them," he says.

Carter reduces risk in the market through diversification even though the downside risk isn't as significant because he's a value investor. "It provides a natural hedge against risk because you're buying stuff that's already cheap," he says. "If the S&P 500 [Standard & Poor's composite index of 500 stocks] is invested 20% in technology, then you should be investing the same amount to minimize risk. We're diversified but not in sync with the market. We have exposure to all sectors."

THE LAST WORD

CARTER SAYS AFRICAN-AMERICANS SHOULD BE cognizant of whom they are spending their money with. "If it comes down to buying toothpaste X or toothpaste Y, find out how each company is impacting your community, and make that part of your purchasing power," Carter says, adding that the role of consumer activist is similar to that of shareholder activist. "African-Americans need to enter the next phase of civil rights, which is economic development. We have to think about where we spend our dollars, where we invest, and how our community benefits. If people bring these issues to bear, they can effect change. It's about acting locally, thinking globally, and using your investment dollars to enrich yourself."

Chapter 13

Pierre Dunagan is an investment officer at First Chicago NBD Investment Services. He currently resides in Chicago, Illinois.

PIERRE DUNAGAN

PIERRE DUNAGAN IS AN INVESTMENT OFFICER WITH First Chicago NBD Investment Services in Chicago, specializing in retirement planning. He's managing $20 million in assets for individuals, and the average net worth of his client base is $100,000.

"I work with people who go through downsizing and early retirement from corporations. They have to move their money from 401(k) plans into IRAs, and they are in somewhat of a crisis situation because they're in their late forties and early fifties and they're not making the kind of money that they made before. So, they have a lot of planning to do around adjusting their expenses and also how to live off what they have," he says.

Prior to First Chicago, Dunagan worked as an associate vice president at Dean Witter.

"When I became an associate vice president at Dean Witter, it was based on my production. It wasn't subjective, so I didn't have that issue. But you did run into racism with clients. You had some whites who didn't want a black person as their broker," he said. "I don't see a lot of blacks in management, but as far as the sale side goes, we're here. A lot of times, unfortunately, we don't last because it's so hard to build up a clientele. The attrition rate—black or white—is extremely high. Generally, to make it in management you start as a broker. So, if you can't make it as a broker, you're probably not going to make it up to management."

FINANCIAL ADVICE: PLAN FOR RETIREMENT

Dunagan says that the goal should be to have enough money saved for retirement so you can live off the interest and not have to disturb the principal, and then pass the principal on to your heirs. "Once you retire, you should have your investments in something that will grow because of inflation. Just because you're retired doesn't mean that the costs of goods and services are going to stop going up. The other thing to consider is that people are living a lot longer than they used to. So, a lot of people are going to live almost as long in retirement as they did when they worked," he says.

In order to build retirement savings that produce interest, Dunagan says people should have a balanced portfolio of stocks and bonds using mutual funds. For a 30-year-old, Dunagan recommends first saving three months of living expenses in a money market account. Once that has been achieved, the next step would be to invest 30% of the assets in CDs or bonds, with the balance invested in four areas of the stock market. The four areas are blue-chip stocks, growth stocks, aggressive growth stocks, and international growth stocks.

"Make sure that each year you rebalance that portfolio to bring it back to those four equal quarters. If one really starts to outperform the others, stay disciplined. Force yourself not to move everything out of one class of assets and into another that's jumping, because that may not be the case the following year," he says.

Even though Dunagan recommends having some of your retirement money in bonds, he says the majority of your growth will come from the stock market. "Within the fixed-income portion of your retirement portfolio, don't use bond mutual funds. If you buy a bond, you know that you're going to get your money back at maturity. You know that you're going to have a set interest rate. But when you buy a bond mutual fund, the money will fluctuate in value and that portion of the portfolio isn't going to be guaranteed," he says.

PERSONAL PORTFOLIO

To prepare for retirement, Dunagan contributes about 12% of his annual income into his 401(k). Aside from that, Dunagan's personal portfolio includes stock investments in Compaq, Motorola, Dean Witter, and R. R. Donnelley & Sons, a printing company. He's also invested in the AIM Value Fund, the Pioneer International Fund, and the Kemper-Dreman High Return Fund, which is a blue-chip stock fund. "Right now my portfolio is 33% in individual stocks and mutual funds. The balance is a third in real estate and a third in collectibles, primarily art. My best friend is a contractor, so I rehabilitate real estate and go for the capital gains. We buy in depressed areas, fix property up, and resell for a capital gain. With artwork, I've been buying Shona sculptures. Shona is a tribe in Zimbabwe, and they make stone sculptures. I've also been buying more contemporary African-American art. The value appreciates, and I've been buying it undervalued," he says.

Dunagan says his current net worth is about $200,000, but he's hoping that in the next five years he'll have a net worth of over a million dollars as a result of his investments in the stock market, real estate, and collectibles.

Dunagan's secret to amassing his current fortune is that he began a disciplined savings program at the young age of 24 years old. "I started putting 10% or 12% of my money in a 401(k), and I put 50% in the company's stock and 50% in a blue-chip stock mutual fund. Over time, it just grew, with stock splits and dividends. Now, I'm putting in the maximum—which is $9,000 a year—and investing primarily in growth stocks," he says.

For people who are self-employed and who don't have

access to a 401(k) plan, Dunagan recommends investing in an IRA or a SEP IRA, both of which are available through mutual fund families. "The beauty of being self-employed is that you have tons of investment options and, if there's a secret to truly retiring successfully, it's being self-employed. Most of the clients I've seen who have million-dollar accounts are people who are self-employed, and if you saw them on the street, you'd never know that a lot of them are as wealthy as they are. And they do retire quite well," he says.

Dunagan saves 10% every pay period in a money market account and tithes 10% to his church. "I adjusted my living expenses to what I take home. Instead of letting my living expenses dictate what I save, I save first and then whatever is left determines the way that I live. That's not to say that I haven't made mistakes. When I was younger I had credit cards and ran them up. I eventually paid that debt down. But as you get older, you begin to take a look at things and you reassess your own portfolio. I never leave more than six months of living expenses in the money market account. At some point, I put the extra money into a mutual fund and then invest it in real estate or a piece of art," he says.

The investment that Dunagan is still reaping benefits from is his stake in Dean Witter stock. He worked there for eight years and invested about $20,000 in stock over the course of that time. Today, his investment is worth about $60,000, he says.

In terms of the performance of the stocks he's purchased, Dunagan has tripled his money with Compaq because it has split three times. He put $5,000 in Compaq, and now it's worth $15,000. "I looked at Compaq and they had back orders of over $100 million for their products. I

NEW IRAS TO CONSIDER

A new retirement plan called SIMPLE-IRA (Savings Incentive Match Program for Employees), enacted under the Small Business Job Protection Act of 1996, allows self-employed persons to put away up to $6,000 a year, a substantial increase over the standard $2,000 contribution limit in an IRA.

Judy Thorp, partner-in-charge of the tax department of Grant Thornton, an international public accounting and management consulting firm in Chicago, says a SIMPLE-IRA plan is a type of 401(k) plan. "It allows you to defer your contribution on a pretax basis and allows the contributions to earn interest on a tax-deferred basis," she says. "Basically, you have all that interest that's being compounded into your account and you're not going to be subject to taxation. That's the two big pluses."

A SIMPLE-IRA plan invests in mutual funds, stocks, and bonds and can be purchased through banks or mutual fund families. For example, Fidelity Investments offers a SIMPLE-IRA mutual fund package that invests in Fidelity no-load funds. Call 800-544-5373 to enroll or visit Fidelity's Internet Web site (http://www.fidelity.com).

Roth IRAs, named after the chair of the Senate Finance Committee, Senator William Roth, Jr., allow you to put away up to $2,000 annually after tax. You never have to pay taxes on it if it's spent on your first house (up to $10,000), used after you reach age 59½ or become disabled, or paid out when you die. You're also allowed to withdraw a sum equal to your contribution tax-free.

To qualify as a single person, your adjusted gross income can't exceed $95,000, and if you're married, your income can't exceed $150,000. Roth IRAs are available through banks, brokers, and mutual fund families.

was looking at the quality of their products, and I looked at the earnings. The earnings were going up every year, which influenced me to buy it," he says.

INVESTING ADVICE: RESEARCH FOR VALUE

Dunagan says he's a value investor, preferring to buy something for less than it's actually worth. He does this by researching stocks or by investing in value-oriented mutual funds, such as the AIM Value Fund. "In the case of stocks I look for a company that's undervalued and look at its price-to-earnings ratio compared to other stocks within the same industry and see if there are any discrepancies. Value Line (212-907-1500) publishes a list of those types of companies. It has a section called undervalued securities," he says.

Dunagan isn't suggesting that you invest in undervalued securities without researching them. He recommends making sure the company is still strong and finding out why the stock is undervalued. "The best-case scenario is that the stock is cheap for short-term reasons, such as experiencing a bad quarter or taking a charge on earnings because of a layoff. Then, it may be presenting value for that reason. The other thing is that sometimes the market goes down and stocks go down with it. The earnings are still strong, but it's just that the market is going down," he says.

Finding out why a stock is cheap requires some research. The way the average person can do this is to go to the library and look at any news stories on the companies. "Generally, there are going to be news stories that will tell you what happened, but there's still some speculation involved. Your assumption may be wrong, but the bottom line is that you have to do your own research and make a decision based on your own feelings. But, it's not a guarantee that the stock is going to work out and come back up just because it's undervalued. Overall, it's less risky to be a value investor. If the market were to take a hit, an undervalued stock won't go as low as a high-flying growth stock," he says.

As far as asset allocation is concerned, Dunagan says a good rule of thumb is to take the first numeral of your age and add a zero to it. The result is the percentage that you should have in fixed-income securities. The balance should be invested in growth stocks and mutual funds. So, for example, if you are 42 years old, 40% of your assets should be in fixed-income securities and 60% should be in the stock market. "The secret is to put away what you can with the goal of eventually being able to live off the interest from your investments," he says. "The S&P 500 over the past 10 years has averaged roughly around 12%, so looking at a good stock mutual fund or a basic S&P 500 index fund is not a guarantee [of a 12% return], but that's what it's done in the past."

Dunagan's recommendation for what to do with a $50,000 inheritance depends on age. For the 45-year-old married couple who owns a home, Dunagan recommends putting the money into mutual funds within a variable annuity. "The advantage of purchasing mutual funds inside the variable annuity is the couple wouldn't have to pay taxes on the capital gains until they took it out when they retire," he says. "It's an insurance contract that gives you the ability to purchase investments inside of it on a tax-deferred basis. It works similarly to an IRA, but you can't write off the money you put into it and you're not limited as to how much you put into a variable annuity. You can put as much as you want in there," he says.

BENEFITS OF A TAX-DEFERRED VARIABLE ANNUITY

A variable annuity is a contract between an insurance company and an individual. The benefit of owning a tax-deferred variable annuity is the potential for above-average returns, because your assets may be invested in the securities markets and assume actual risk. If the annuity contract meets certain conditions of the Internal Revenue Code, then the earnings, if left in the variable annuity, are not taxed. The objective is to let the annuity increase in value and accumulate tax-deferred until you surrender the contract or annuitize it.

Since a variable annuity is a security, a prospectus must be given to you with or preceding a specific proposal. The prospectus provides information about the investment choices, the risks, and the variable annuity itself.

Source: The Investing Kit by Bay Gruber, © 1996 by Dearborn Financial Publishing, Inc. Published by Dearborn Financial Publishing, Inc. All rights reserved. Reprinted with permission.

The pitfalls of investing, according to Dunagan, are greed and fear. As far as greed is concerned, Dunagan recommends avoiding putting too much money in one stock that's doing well. To combat fear, Dunagan says avoid selling stock when the market is going down. Instead, try to roll with the punches of a fluctuating market. "Avoid being shortsighted or too short-term–oriented," he says.

THE LAST WORD

DUNAGAN SAYS THAT AFRICAN-AMERICANS HAVE increased their knowledge of investing, but they need to get past investing just in CDs and fixed-income investments, especially when it comes to saving for retirement.

"Say good-bye to the bank and look at the stock market and municipal bonds, where the interest is tax-free. I would say begin saving for retirement early, because the earlier you begin, the quicker you are able to get where you need to be. If you're working and participating in a 401(k), put away 10% of your income within that 401(k). The other thing is, I would map out the type of retirement that you want to have. So, if you want to have a second home in Arizona, I would find out how much that would cost. If you want to do a lot of traveling and see the world, I would save for something like that," he says.

Chapter 14

Hamilton Lewis is president, founder, and owner of Hamilton Lewis Capital Management, Inc. He received his B.A. in finance and B.S. in management from Houston Baptist University. He currently resides in Houston, Texas, with his wife and three children.

HAMILTON LEWIS

HAMILTON LEWIS CAME TO AMERICA FROM LIBERIA, West Africa, with $400 and a dream that he would become somebody. "I could not be who I am today in Liberia," he says. Lewis says he's three generations from the freed American slaves who founded Liberia in 1847.

"I had no fear in coming over here," Lewis says. "I just knew. I could envision myself going to an American university." After attending Houston Baptist University on a full basketball scholarship (Lewis is six foot eight), he graduated and worked for Merrill Lynch as a stockbroker for six years. In 1991, he started his own firm, Hamilton Lewis Capital Management, in Houston.

It's important to note that Lewis believes in the power of visualization and meditation. He says he spends 10 minutes meditating both in the morning and at night on a daily basis. "I bring my fantasy into reality by operating the right hemisphere of my brain. You instruct yourself and suggest to yourself with pictures. Tell the right hemisphere who you are and what you want to become. I recommend meditating on God's word twice a day. I've been doing so since April 21, 1979, and it works for me," he says.

While Lewis worked at Merrill Lynch, he was steadily saving his money so he could open his own business. When he opened his business from home six years ago, he had $70,000 in the bank. He started out with $3 million in assets, because some of his clients from Merrill Lynch elected to follow him. Today, he has close to $30 million under management. "In the first year, I made $34,000, which was a loss because I spent probably $60,000 on equipment. The second year was profitable. I made $120,000," he says.

Lewis caters to high net worth individuals. He has

about 150 clients with an average account worth $250,000. The minimum amount that he will accept to invest is $100,000. "My clients are presidents of small- to medium-sized companies. I have professional people, such as lawyers and CPAs and a lot of doctors, some Hispanic doctors and American doctors. Five million is the average net worth of my clients," he says.

Lewis says adamantly that he's a money manager, not a broker. He is accredited as a Certified Financial Planner and Chartered Market Technician, which is the highest recognition someone can have in the world of technical analysis. "My net worth is more than $400,000. Most of it has come from the appreciation of my business, which is worth $1.5 million. But, I probably won't sell it now because I'm waiting for a different market cycle to come by, maybe in the year 2006.

Lewis says $300,000 of his net worth comes from his business, and the remaining $100,000 is his investment in Cisco Systems. He initially bought 1,000 shares at $18 in November 1991. The price of the stock is now $68, and since then Lewis has purchased 2,000 more shares.

Surprisingly, Cisco is the only stock that Lewis owns. He says he bought it because he noticed a lot of changes in its daily trading volume. "The number of shares trading was higher than normal, which means that big money was flowing in. Once I started seeing an increase in volume, I paid attention because that's a sign that money is flowing into the stocks, which means that very soon the price will move a lot higher. The big secret is to follow the money because it's aware of what's going on. You can spot the big money by the number of shares being traded," he says.

"The reason we own only Cisco is because if you really know something you jump in two feet deep. By concentrating one's assets in as few stocks as possible, the family has a tendency to generate incredible amounts of money. I say concentrate because I have a client with a million dollars invested in only three stocks, and his portfolio is growing at 60% a year. So, if we can grow an asset base at 60% a year, it means we know something or are guessing right," he says.

For most finance experts, diversification is the mantra. But, Lewis is the exception to the rule. He prefers concentrating in a few stocks, not diversifying across the board. "Concentration forces you to focus and not try to become everything to everyone. There are more than 6,000 stocks that trade and you can't pay attention to all of them. Narrow it down to the top 10 and pick one you can fall in with for a long period of time. Expose your capital to those positions and you have a chance to make significant dollars," he says.

In addition to concentrating, Lewis recommends that investors focus on the 10 most actively traded stocks (which he does for his clients) on the New York Stock Exchange (NYSE) and then subsequently on the NASDAQ market. "Do some research on the 10 most actively traded stocks on the NYSE, pick a company, and then acquire shares of that company. I say the top 10 because the active trading indicates that people are parking money into these stocks. There's a table of the top 10 in *Investor's Business Daily*. Start with the New York Stock Exchange, because it has more liquidity. Later, you can switch to the NASDAQ market, which has high-flying companies that are growing by more than 30% a year. But start with the NYSE to gain confidence before getting into the fast lane," he says.

Equally important is knowing when to bail out of the

market, says Lewis. You need to get your money out before the market declines, but figuring out when the market is going down is difficult. Lewis has a strategy: "You'll know that by looking at the price of your stock once a week. If the price is $59 one week, $69 the next week, and then the third week it dips below a previous low, you know you have trouble and you should exit the market. If you don't, you won't have any additional monies to generate capital with," he says.

Even though Lewis's minimum investment is $100,000, he says that anyone with $50 can benefit from the market. "A person doesn't have to open a business to amass wealth in America. You can start with $50 a month and make a fortune. If you are diligent, you can participate in the success of the market. The key is finding a stock you like. Call the company and get an annual report. Get to know the investor relations people at the company. Get press releases from the company and pay attention to the daily prices that you see in the paper. You can purchase the stock either through a discount broker or, in some cases, directly from the company. Just make certain that the stock is in the top 10 of the most actively traded stocks," he says.

Some of Lewis's favorite stocks that he has bought for his clients are familiar ones. Ninety percent of his stock picks have split, which doubles the amount of shares you own in a company. He bought General Electric in 1994 for $54 a share. It went up to $120 a share and split two-for-one. Now, it's trading at $61 a share. The same goes for Coca-Cola: Lewis bought it in July 1994 at $36 a share. The stock went up to $82 and then split. Currently, it's priced at $68 a share. Both McDonald's and Microsoft have split, too. "Splits are attractive because they increase the number of shares you own. I don't concern myself with splits. I just make sure that the company is on an upswing. If it splits, that's just a bonus. Usually, once the price gets too high and expensive for the average investor, the company splits the stock and that allows average people to come in and buy again," he says.

Lewis uses technical analysis versus fundamental analysis when it comes to picking stock. He says he looks for higher highs and lower lows by checking out the four prices listed in the paper. They include the opening price, the closing price, the high, and the low. "Make sure the low is always higher than the previous day's low and today's high should be higher than yesterday's high. This is technical. As long as we get that, that's a buy signal. That's what the public needs to pay attention to, the technical analysis. You're looking for a pattern formation," he says.

WAYS TO ANALYZE STOCKS

Fundamental analysis uses corporate records to forecast a stock's performance. The information examined includes the company's management, history, earnings, balance sheet, and products. Lewis says fundamental analysis is a process of looking at the bigger picture, such as the impact of the economy and politics.

Technical analysis uses the history of the stock's price and the psychology of the markets. Investing decisions using technical analysis are based on the price patterns, statistics, trading volume, probability, trading ranges, and market cyles. Lewis equates it to mathematics.

In addition to technical analysis, Lewis also selects stocks based on industry and sector rotation. "I buy the best performing stock in the best performing industry," he says. His favorite sectors include the local area network (LAN), mini- and microcomputer, and software sectors of the technology industry, and the funeral services industry. Stocks he mentioned include Cisco, 3Com, Xylan, Ascend Communications, Microsoft, Computer Associates, Compaq, Dell Computer, Hewlett Packard, and Service Corporation International, a funeral services company in Houston.

Unlike many money managers, Lewis prefers to buy puts or sell calls. "A put is an option contract that gives me the right to sell my stock at a higher price, sort of like a guarantee. It's not worth buying puts unless you have at least $10,000 or $20,000 invested; then you can consider protecting it. When you sell a call, you are speculating in the market. If you notice higher highs, you can buy a call contract on the underlying stock for anywhere from $200 to $3,900 each. It's the quickest way to make a lot of money," he says.

Lewis says investors must buy something that they can sell easily to avoid the pitfalls of investing. "Stay away from things that are thinly traded and penny stocks, things that are cheap. Avoid participating in wide spreads. You do that by looking at the bid and the asking price. If the spread between the two is too wide, you have few players in that stock, which means that you might not be able to sell it. You might not find a buyer. If they are actively traded stocks, you don't have to worry about the bid price because you know it's liquid. It's the cream of the crop. Twelve and a half cents to 25 cents is a reasonable spread," he says. "If penny stocks are not in the top 10 actively traded issues, I don't want to be there. If the top 10 change, you change accordingly. You must be flexible at the same time that you are investing consistently."

PERSONAL PORTFOLIO

When it comes to saving, Lewis puts away about $1,000 a month, or 5% of his income. But, all of it is invested in Cisco stock. He doesn't put any money into a savings account. In fact, Lewis doesn't even have a bank account. Instead, he maintains cash management accounts with Merrill Lynch and Schwab. "They are nonbank banks, earning interest on the balances. The minimum is $20,000, and you get a Visa card, a checking account, and a detailed statement each month. The advantage is that it keeps track of every penny and reduces the amount of paperwork by having all your assets in one central location. You also receive tax-free interest on your money market accounts, about 3%," he says. "In addition, you get access to a financial consultant who helps you to answer questions about whatever you want to know. They send you company research about stock you're interested in."

INVESTING ADVICE: CHOOSE YOUR SECTORS

Lewis says investors should have money allocated in, at the most, three sectors. "Have in total about three or four stocks with one or two stocks from each sector. You want to make sure the stocks have greater relative performance to the marketplace. To figure that, take the price of the stock and divide it by the price of the index. The greater number you have, the better the stock you have. You know the stock is outperforming the index. If the number starts to decline, get out of the stock," he says.

With a $50,000 inheritance, Lewis says you should take a chance and invest all of it in the market. "Divide it by five so you have five units of $10,000, and invest two units of $10,000 until you gain confidence. Look at the beverage sector, restaurants, technology, and the conglomerate sector. Invest in three major companies, and sit back and watch your monies grow. Then, you can start adding more dollars to the market," hc says.

THE LAST WORD

LEWIS SAYS AFRICAN-AMERICANS NEED TO RElease their money to the stock market after increasing their knowledge about the markets. He says that at least 10% of your income should be invested in the stock market and whatever you're saving should be put into a stock market account.

"African-Americans need to know that they can make it in this society. They need to consistently increase their knowledge about the free enterprise system by reading books about finance, money markets, Wall Street, and how the United States works," he says.

Chapter 15

John Rogers is president of Ariel Capital Management. He received his B.A. from Princeton University. He currently resides in Chicago, Illinois, with his wife and daughter.

JOHN ROGERS

JOHN ROGERS MAY SEEM SHY AND UNASSUMING BUT this 38 year old has a net worth of more than $10 million. In fact, in 1994 he was featured in *Time* magazine as one of 50 future leaders under 40.

During our meeting, Rogers said he had been reading an article in *George* magazine about Rahm Emanuel, senior adviser to President Clinton for policy and strategy, with whom Rogers worked on Richard Daley's mayoral election campaign in Chicago. "It's interesting to see where people's careers take them and where they end up," he observed.

Rogers's own career contains a host of firsts. He founded the first African-American institutional money management firm, Ariel Capital Management, a decade and a half ago. Ariel was also the first black company to start a mutual fund (in 1986), and Ariel's mutual funds are the only African-American ones that are priced daily in the newspaper. The firm manages $1.6 billion; $350 million of this is invested in Ariel's three mutual funds: Ariel Growth, Ariel Appreciation, and Ariel Premier Bond Fund. The firm's clients are mainly big pension funds. Their corporate clients include Ford Motor Company, AT&T, and United Airlines.

Rogers says that being the first black doesn't bother him. "There are some advantages and disadvantages to being black. The positive is that you have the opportunity to be a pioneer. The tough side is that some people don't like to see us succeed," he says.

Rogers hasn't let anything get in the way of his success. He started his career working for William Blair & Company in Chicago for two and a half years as a broker. During that time, he grew interested in money management and mutual funds. "I didn't think they'd hire me to do that. I was a broker and they saw me as a broker," he says. "At William Blair everything was there under one roof. So, I got a chance to observe all of the departments and how they work; and I realized that my personality fit better in money management and mutual funds, because I was developing a long-term investment philosophy. In the brokerage business, you get paid per transaction, while in money management you get paid a fee to manage assets. So, being in the investment counseling side of the business allows you to take a long-term perspective."

Eager to start managing money, he started his own firm when he was only 24 years old. To find investors for his company, he appealed to his parents, family friends, and former clients from his brokerage days. "I told them the story about the opportunities that would be out there in the world for a high-quality African-American–owned money management firm. We raised a little over $250,000 in seed capital to get the company started," he says. "I had a good idea at the right time. There had never been an African-American–owned institutional money management firm in this country."

On a typical day, Rogers arrives at the office at 6:45 A.M. to read research on companies. He'll have a power breakfast at around 7:30 A.M. with politicians, bankers, and civic leaders. Throughout the day, he'll either meet with clients, talk to prospective clients, or do some community work.

Rogers works out every day, playing basketball and lifting weights. In the evenings, he'll usually go to cocktail receptions or dinner parties. He goes home about 9:30 P.M.

Rogers believes that being first in a field gives you a leg up. He also believes that people accumulate wealth in this country by starting their own business. He says his business is the single most important investment he made that he is still reaping benefits from. "My net worth is tied up in my company," he says. "Secondly, the next big chunk of my assets are tied up in my company's mutual fund. The Ariel Growth Fund is where I have my money. It's been a good investment for us." Rogers puts about 20% of his salary into savings every month, which is split between investing in his own mutual fund and adding to his seven-year-old daughter's education fund.

Community outreach is a major part of Rogers's entrepreneurial life. He serves as the chairman of the board of the Chicago Park District. Several years ago he also adopted a class of 40 sixth graders to follow through college as part of the I Have a Dream Foundation. Rogers spends well over $200,000 a year for the program and he anticipates helping to pay for college for 30 of the 40 students. The students, who are currently seniors in high school, received financial help from Rogers to attend private schools in Chicago.

Rogers is concerned with education in other areas as well. He has undertaken the task of trying to educate the African-American public about investing in mutual funds, because the black community has not been as receptive to mutual funds as whites. "We've been trying to change that by advertising every month in *Black Enterprise* and using Tom Burrell's creative marketing advertising to reach our community. We've been sponsors at various trade organizations like the black MBA conference every year and this year at the black journalists conference. We're going to continue to do that to reach out to our community to get people excited about investing in mutual funds."

PERSONAL PORTFOLIO

Aside from the stocks in his mutual funds, Rogers generally doesn't invest in stocks. "My personal portfolio is invested in my own mutual fund, the Ariel Growth Fund, my company, and my home," he says. The only stock he owns is Aon, the largest insurance brokers in the world. It's not surprising that he owns the stock because he sits on the board of directors.

INVESTING ADVICE: KEEP IT SIMPLE

In Rogers's opinion, the perfect asset allocation is 50% to 60% in stocks through mutual funds, 25% to 30% in real estate, and the rest in money market funds or bonds for safety or conservatism. In other words, investing doesn't have to be fancy or overly diversified. "I would keep it simple. I'm not into putting money everywhere. I'm not interested in the futures market, commodities, or tax shelters. Focus on common stocks, conservative money markets, and real estate," he says. "If you get into your seventies and you're thinking about retiring, you might want to be more conservative and pull money out of the stock market and put it into bonds, where you get a guaranteed fixed return."

To get a 10% to 12% return on a yearly basis, you have to be invested in common stock or common stock mutual funds. "It's tough to do," Rogers says. "There's no formula. You basically have to find good businesses that have proven they can grow 10% to 12% a year; and, basically, stock prices are going to follow the growth rate of the businesses. So, you have to find those companies out there that are growing and buy them at the right price before everyone discovers how great they are. You have to get in there early. If you get in too late, the price is going to reflect all that good news."

Rogers is adamant about investing in common stocks and mutual funds. His firm commissioned the independent research firm Roper Starch Worldwide to conduct a national investment survey. The survey shows that African-Americans are more conservative and risk-averse than non-African-Americans. Rogers says that as a community African-Americans are underinvested.

African-Americans tend to have less diversified investments and invest less in mutual funds, stocks, and bonds. For example, according to the study, 22% of blacks invest in mutual funds compared to 35% of whites. About 27% of blacks invest in stocks and bonds compared to 38% of whites. Even though African-Americans don't invest as aggressively, they tend to seek higher returns than whites. The study found that African-Americans seek average annual returns of 14.7% compared to 11.2% return for whites.

To achieve higher average annual returns, Rogers recommends setting aside at least 10% to 15% of your salary for investing. "The way to get long-term returns is to be invested in equities. We're too conservative," he says. "We invest but we typically put our money in money market funds and bank CDs, and we keep our money in the bank. We have to get out of that mode, because in the long run you end up giving up a lot of wealth accumulation if you invest too conservatively. African-Americans need to invest like everyone else."

Rogers's investing style is conservative. He's more inclined to do his homework and try to find a stable company to invest in, in order to reduce risk. This philosophy spills over into his job as a mutual fund manager. Rogers is more likely to own Clorox, the bleach company, rather than Microsoft, the technology company. He says investors should understand what they're investing in. "Don't trust too many people," he says. "And don't invest in things you don't know a lot about. Sticking with a few things is important. People want to get involved in so many things at once. The best way to lose money is to go chasing after every hot deal. Instead, just stick with a few things that you know well."

Rogers says investing in things you don't understand is one of the pitfalls of investing. He strongly advises staying away from hot trends and tips. "People race out and buy high-tech funds because they read about them. But you have to look forward and make educated decisions about the future," he says. One way to make educated decisions is by reading about investing as much as possible. Rogers reads *Forbes*, *BusinessWeek*, *Black Enterprise*, and *Barron's* as well as books on investing. He recommends reading books on Warren Buffett's investing style.

REAL ESTATE INVESTMENT TRUSTS (REITS)

Similar to mutual funds, REITs are an indirect method of investing in real estate. REITs pool money from investors and invest in properties. You can sell and buy shares anytime just like with stocks. The yields on REITs can range from 6% to 12% annually. Their share prices rise and fall with the stock market. It's best to take a long-term approach with this investment vehicle. Plan on holding your shares for three to five years.

One of Rogers's strategies is investing in real estate investment trusts (REITs). "REITs are a good inflation hedge. One we've looked at is Merryland in Maryland and the Rouse Company, which is not a REIT, but they own a mall in Baltimore and the South Street Seaport in New York City. They're big mall developers, and it's a good way to play the real estate markets," he says.

As fund manager of the Ariel Growth Fund, Rogers says he is a value investor, which means that he tries to find stocks that are selling at low prices relative to their expected earnings and profits. Ariel's special brand of value investing involves focusing more on company management and products than most of their competition. He looks for companies that have proven they have a strong brand name and the ability to grow their earnings in a consistent fashion. Rogers wants to buy companies that are

---

INVESTING IN REITS

To invest in a real estate investment trust (REIT), ask your stockbroker to invest directly. The Merryland and Investment Company, Inc. (706-722-6756) owns apartments throughout the Southeast. Its share price was $20.50 on March 27, 1997. The Rouse Company (410-992-6546) is a real estate acquisition and development company whose properties include Faneuil Hall Marketplace in Boston and Harbor Place in downtown Baltimore.

Short of investing directly in a REIT, you can invest in mutual funds that invest in REITs. Consider Longleaf Partners, which manages the Longleaf Realty Fund (901-761-2474). The minimum investment is $10,000.

DIVIDEND REINVESTMENT PLANS (DRIPS)

Some companies allow you to purchase stock directly from the company without a broker. No-load stocks are available from more than 90 U.S. corporations. You can make an initial stock purchase and then enroll in the company's dividend reinvestment plan (DRIP) to buy subsequent shares. The minimum investment can be anywhere from $25 to $1,000. For example, Bob Evans Farms (614-492-4952) asks for an initial investment of $50, while Dial Corporation (800-453-2235) asks for $100.

To find out which companies have a no-load stock program, write for a free list from DRIP Investor Newsletter, 7412 Calumet Avenue, Hammond, IN 46324, or call the No-Load Stock Clearinghouse at 800-774-4117.

good at what they do, cheap relative to their profits, and not subject to the volatility that creates risk. For example, the Ariel Growth Fund is invested in Clorox Company, First Brands Corporation, Hasbro Inc., Bob Evans Farms, Inc., and Century Telephone Enterprises.

"The stocks we consider are not subject to the volatility that you find in the technology markets or in the cyclical industries," he says. "The second thing is, we focus on the quality of people who run the businesses we invest in. We try to get a sense of the integrity and work habits and the motivations of the management team. We spend a lot of time trying to determine the quality of the products that are being produced by going out in the field and testing products ourselves. We find out whether the products add value to the customers or not. I think it's something that everyone can do if you stick to an industry you know well and get out there and test the products yourself. A lot of people just don't do a good job of that." Testing products is as simple as going to the mall and looking at products or sampling electronic merchandise at a store like The Sharper Image.

THE LAST WORD

ROGERS SAYS AFRICAN-AMERICANS NEED TO BE-come aggressive investors because of retirement's changing landscape. "African-Americans have to invest money—that's the bottom line. We have to have our money working for us. It's more important than ever because Social Security might not be with us forever," he says. "There's a real threat to Social Security, and more corporations are getting rid of the old-fashioned defined-benefit pension plan and going more toward the modern 401(k) plan. So you've got to make your own investment decisions and start putting away money on your own, or you might not be able to retire in the style that your parents did or that your peers are doing."

Chapter 16

Steven Sanders is president and CEO of Sanders Financial. He received his B.B.A. from Howard University. He currently resides in Voorhees, New Jersey, with his wife and son.

STEVEN SANDERS

STEVEN SANDERS IS PRESIDENT AND CEO OF SANDERS Financial, an investment advisory firm whose average portfolio is about $85,000. He started the firm in the basement of his parents' home with a partner back in 1986 with about $6,000 that he'd saved from working at Mellon Bank as a commercial credit analyst and at Aetna in the employee benefits division.

"The job at Aetna gave me great training and I had to get my securities licenses, which allowed me to have those licenses right out of college. Mellon gave me a background in how to read and analyze financial statements," he says.

After leaving corporate America, he lived on the $6,000 and some revenues from his firm for about two and a half years before turning a profit. His clients came through connections with Howard University, his alma mater. Sanders gave seminars to black sororities, fraternities, and churches. "There was basically no money to take out as salaries. We were just able to pay bills on time. Any excess was put back into the business," he says. "We were recommending mutual fund portfolios to individuals. We were investment advisers. We did the investment side of financial planning, and made money from investment advisory fees and mutual fund commissions. We'd recommend products based on the need that fit a particular client."

Sanders started the business because he saw a need in the marketplace. "Mutual funds were becoming the investment of choice, and individuals didn't know how to use them wisely or didn't understand them at all. I thought that the African-American community was being underserved when it came to understanding investment vehicles. So, I carved it out as a niche," he says.

Sanders has since expanded his business. In addition

to the investment advisory firm, he started Finedco, a financial education business, in 1992, and MDL Capital Management, an institutional money-management firm, in 1995. "A lot of my net worth is tied up in my businesses. It's not in actual cash dollars—it's the value of my businesses. So, that would make it worth several million, close to about $3 million," he says.

Sanders prides himself on the fact that he's invested most of his money back into his businesses. "If I had a little left over in savings and one of the businesses had a need, instead of borrowing from a bank, I'd use my own personal savings to plow it back into the business," he says.

Sanders studied wealthy people for years, trying to figure out why they have the amounts of money they have versus nonwealthy people. He devised the Spending Plan of Action System idea.

"I wondered why there was such a great divide between the haves and the have-nots, and I got a chance to see that some of the wealthy people were not always born into wealth. It wasn't that they were smarter than anyone else. They just decided to apply some basic principles," he says. "I began to notice that wealthy people were using the system of paying themselves first and then spending last. They were constantly saving first and spending last, whereas nonwealthy people were always spending first and then trying to save last. The problem was, nonwealthy people never had enough left over to save. Paying yourself first means putting away at least 10%. It sounds more complicated than it is but you actually become a bill yourself."

Sanders is realistic. He says if it's not 10% a month then establish an empty piggy bank or jar in which you can deposit your pocket change. Even this adds up, he reasons.

"If you can't afford to put away 10%, try 5% or 1%. I don't care if it's just a dollar a day. It begins to add up," he says.

Creating a Spending Plan of Action would help to cure the spender's disease, which is spending every dime that you earn. "We need to learn how to hold onto the money a little longer than we're holding onto it now. Once you've learned how to hold onto it, what you're doing is changing the entire system around from paying everyone else to paying yourself first. You pay yourself first by saving and investing some of your money, whether it's in mutual funds or 401(k) plans," he says.

The Spending Plan of Action involves looking at how much you're earning individually at a micro level, both before-tax and after-tax income. "We need to understand the difference between our gross and net paychecks. We can't spend our gross checks. We can spend only what we earn after taxes. We need to look very closely at exactly how we are spending our money. You basically make a list of all your monthly expenses and then prioritize the list," he says. "Some are needs and some are wants. The needs should be at the top of the list and the wants should be at the bottom. Pay off your needs first and then focus on wants. This is a Spending Plan of Action System, which has been used for thousands of years by people to help control their personal finances."

Another savings strategy is an employer's 401(k) plan, because the employer will usually match a portion of your contribution, and the contributions grow tax-deferred. Sanders says many African-Americans invest too conservatively in their 401(k) plans. "It's a great way to accumulate mass wealth inside of the capitalistic system that we participate in. We need to know how to invest our money inside our 401(k) plan. We need to diversify our portfolios better so we can participate in the increases in the stock market that are yet to occur, which means shifting from safe vehicles and taking more risk in the portfolio," he says. "Your 401(k) will be one of your greatest assets going forward. If you use it properly, the amount of money accumulated will more than likely be greater than the equity built up in your home. In the past, we've viewed the home as the greatest asset. But this has changed with the advent of mutual funds and 401(k) plans."

Within the 401(k), instead of investing in guaranteed investment contracts (GICs), money market funds, or very safe bond funds, Sanders recommends investing in more aggressive vehicles such as company stock or stock mutual funds. A GIC works like a CD except that it is a contract issued by an insurance company that gives you a guaranteed rate for a 12-month period. The rate is generally one or two percentage points above inflation.

"A lot of people are participating in the company stock-matching option but not enough in the stock mutual funds options that are available. That could be anything from an S&P 500 index fund to a very aggressive growth mutual fund to an international stock fund. You would be doubling your rate of return inside a 401(k) by moving from the low-risk investment options into higher-return and higher-risk investment options. Instead of earning a 5% to 6% average rate of return, you could earn 9% to 12% annually in the portfolio. That could probably double or triple the amount of money over a 15-year or 20-year time frame," he says. "Even people who are five years away from retiring should still have about 10% to 20% of their portfolios in equities. Even *after* they retire, they should still have 10% to 20% in equities."

An advantage to having a 401(k) plan is that you can borrow from it at a favorable interest rate. Another is tax-deferred growth. "You cannot underestimate the value of tax-deferred growth, which is what's happening with the 401(k). You get a chance to cut your overall income taxes. The money you put into a 401(k) comes off your gross income, before you are taxed. So, it lowers your overall taxable income," he points out.

PERSONAL PORTFOLIO

Sanders himself saves 10% a month. Part of his savings plan for the past 11 years has been investing in mutual funds. He started out dollar cost averaging $25 a month, which is about $1 a day. (Dollar cost averaging is a system of buying securities at regular intervals with a fixed dollar amount.) "I had that deducted from my checking account each month and deposited into an aggressive growth mutual fund, and as my earnings increased, I increased my monthly contribution. I started in 1986, a year before the stock market crash of 1987, but I didn't let the crash stop me. Instead of pulling out, I was scouring for more money to put in at that time. That was probably one of the greatest buying opportunities over the last 10 to 12 years," he says. "This is where I basically accumulated some of the money to plow back into the businesses."

Sanders says the biggest investment that he's still reaping benefits from is the $6,000 he poured into Sanders Financial. "The money that I used in 1986 to start Sanders is now worth about $600,000 or $700,000, if I had to peg a value on it. That investment in Sanders Financial led to Finedco, which led to MDL, the institutional money management firm," he says.

In addition to his businesses, Sanders is invested in four mutual funds, including the Sierra Trust Fund, Ariel Growth Fund, and New England Growth Fund. Although he was not invested in any individual stocks at the time of our interview, Sanders said he was preparing to invest about $2,000 in a little-known technology company called Safeguard Scientifics, which returned 326% to its investors in 1995. In 1996 the stock's return was 35% and year-to-date in 1997 it was 16%, according to Sanders.

Part of his job as president of Sanders Financial is picking stocks for his institutional and retail clients. His investing technique involves looking at what's happening in the economy and anticipating where it might go. For example, if interest rates are low, Sanders reasons that people will get a mortgage to buy a home, which will lead them to want to fix up their home. In that case, Sanders says he would invest in hardware companies like Home Depot. "After I look at the economy and figure out where it might go, I come down to the micro level and look at the industry, which leads me to the leaders of the industry, and I try to anticipate what will happen in the next three to five years. Then I pick stocks," he says. "We're looking for industry leaders, companies that are undervalued, overlooked, and ignored. We're poised to take advantage of any industry that's out of favor or any population trends. For example, the aging of the population today leads us to look at nursing home company stock."

Other criteria for picking stock includes making sure companies are being innovators and not followers. "We check to see that earnings are improving and that the company is finding ways to bring in new customer bases. One of the questions we ask is if the company has a particular niche that they own," he says.

INVESTING ADVICE: DON'T PUT ALL YOUR EGGS IN ONE BASKET

Sanders says investors should use an asset allocation approach to investing, which means not having all your eggs in one basket. "Ninety-two percent of the return of your portfolio is going to come from how your assets are allocated. The different asset categories include cash, stocks, bonds, real estate, and even precious metals. Figure out which percentage of your portfolio should be allocated to each one of those asset categories," he says. "The secret to investing is being in the market consistently and not being overweighted in one particular area or stock. You have to de-emotionalize the investment process. Don't fall in love with one particular stock."

The perfect asset allocation for a 45-year-old—"I'd say put 60% to 80% in stocks, and 10% to 20% in bonds, and no more than 5% in cash. Of the stocks, 10% of the 80% should be in international stocks, 65% should be in aggressive growth stocks, and the remainder should be in blue-chip stocks," he says.

In order to garner 10% to 12% returns, Sanders recommends using mutual funds. His preferred asset mix is about 50% to 70% in stocks, about 30% in government bonds (10% in short-term government bonds), and 10% in high-yield bonds. Before investing, though, Sanders recommends taking a risk tolerance quiz (see Appendix B). "That will set you on the right path to determining what your portfolio should look like. Your score will match up with an asset allocation," he says.

With a hypothetical $50,000 inheritance, Sanders recommends paying off debt first and then investing the rest of the money in seven to ten different mutual funds. With five years or more before retiring, Sanders advises investing 70% to 80% in equity mutual funds, and the rest in government bond funds.

Sanders warns investors to look at the cost of their investments. "African-Americans have chased fast, high rates of return, but we have to be patient and stop looking for a fast turnaround, the quick fast buck. We should be wary of the slick, fast salespeople who are trying to part us from our money," he says. "You also want to look at the cost of investing, outside of the risk. Consider the expenses involved in investing, such as a mutual fund's expense ratio."

Having only $50 a month to invest is no excuse not to invest, Sanders says. He recommends investing $25 in a stock mutual fund and $25 in a bond fund. He also advises first-time investors to watch finance programs on cable channels. "Unlike 10 years ago, there's a proliferation of investment and finance programs that cost you nothing. Subscribe to these programs. Commit to watching them for half an hour a day and channel surf to get an explanation of things. It's the least expensive way to get started," he says.

THE LAST WORD

IF THERE'S ONE THING SANDERS WANTS AFRICAN-Americans to know, it's that personal finance isn't that hard: "It's not as difficult to understand the ABCs of personal finance. Many of us believe that it is. You really just need to spend a little bit of time asking the right questions of the right people—and therein lies your start to controlling the fortunes that you are going to earn."

Chapter 17

Charles Self is senior vice president and director, fixed income at ABN AMRO Asset Management. He received his B.S.B. from the University of Minnesota and M.B.A. from the University of Chicago. He currently resides in Wheaton, Illinois, with his wife and two children.

CHUCK SELF

CHUCK SELF OVERSEES THE MANAGEMENT OF $3.5 billion in equity and bond portfolios at ABN AMRO Asset Management in Chicago. He worked his way up in the finance industry from investment officer at Northern Trust Company to his present position of senior vice president and chief investment officer at ABN AMRO.

"I just decided to do whatever they asked me to do and go in the direction in which people thought my talents would take me. Eventually, as I went on in my career, the focus became fixed income securities. I have a strong quantitative background and I have a liking for the economy and the macroeconomic part of finance and that has the most direct application to fixed income," he says. "I was fortunate in this situation to start as a vice president and become a senior vice president. I started as director of fixed income, which I am today but had the title of chief investment officer added."

If there's one thing that Self wants people to know about the bond market, it is that the bond market is driven purely by inflationary expectations. "When people think that the inflation rate is going to go up, then interest rates go up. When participants think that inflation is going to go down, then interest rates go down. So on the fixed income side, it's our job to figure out what's going to happen to inflationary expectations," he says. "It's much more difficult for the individual to get a good deal at a fair price in the bond market compared to stocks. Most bonds are traded between institutions—about 95%. But with the stock market, the individual can go to a central exchange and buy individual stocks and pay a reasonable commission. That's just not the case in the bond market."

PERSONAL PORTFOLIO

Self's most important investment had nothing to do with bonds. Instead, it was gold that gave him a huge profit. Self invested in gold and precious metals stocks while he was a student. "From the profits of that investment, I bought my wife's engagement ring. That's an investment I'm still reaping benefits from today," he laughs. "I bought gold coins and gold and silver bars from coin dealers. I also owned some gold shares through a mutual fund. We're talking about a thousand-dollar investment or something like that. I tripled my money. It was that one point in time when we had hyperinflation and people became interested in precious metals all of a sudden, and I was fortunate enough to have been there when the run-up in prices occurred."

More recently, when he thought interest rates were very high, Self invested in zero-coupon Treasury strip bonds. "From the end of 1994 to the end of 1995, during that one-year period of time, long-term interest rates went from almost 8% down to 6%, and I made 75% on my money," Self says. "I was buying the principal payment that's due in the year 2020. I bought it at 10 cents to the dollar and if I had held it until maturity, I would have gotten a thousand dollars back for my $100. Since interest rates went down, one year later, it was worth $170, or $17 for every $100. So, that's how I got the 75% return." Bonds are quoted as a percent of 100. If it's priced at $17, for every $1000 bond you own, you'd pay $170.

He cashed in his zero coupons and is no longer invested in them. "I don't recommend it for the average person and I don't recommend it today either because interest rates are relatively low. You want to do it only when you think interest rates are extraordinarily high, because if you're wrong you can lose a lot of money very quickly, too."

Self says the key to his increase in wealth has been that he's very diversified. About 50% of his portfolio is invested in bonds and 50% in stocks. Furthermore, about 50% of his stocks are in international securities, and the other 50% are in domestic securities. On the bond side, he's almost strictly invested in bond funds except for a few Treasury securities. The mutual funds he's invested in belong to his company, ABN AMRO. They include the Rembrandt Growth Fund, the Rembrandt Small Capitalization Fund, Rembrandt International Equity Fund, the Rembrandt Fixed Income Fund, and the Rembrandt Value Fund. He's also invested in a natural resources fund that's not affiliated with his company. The United Services Global Resources Fund invests in oil, gas, and gold mining companies.

Self labels himself a conservative investor except on the fixed income side. "When I feel strongly, I might buy zero-coupon strips. But, I have other things that I want to do in life than look at investment markets, which is what I do all day long. So, mutual funds is the easy way for me to stay invested and diversified," he says.

INVESTING ADVICE: INCLUDE BONDS IN YOUR PORTFOLIO

Despite the high commissions, Self says African-Americans need to make sure that their investment portfolios are diversified to include bonds. "Even though the stock market has done very well in recent years and it has been the place to be, there's no guarantee that the stock market will continue to do as well. And if history is a guide, it's not likely to do as well going forward, and there are many people who think the bond market is going to do better in future years. Because you never know, it's important to have fixed income instruments and fixed income funds as part of your financial plan and a small amount in money market funds to make sure you have liquidity and a low-risk way of saving," he says.

Self says the easiest way to invest in bonds is to own intermediate bonds or be invested in an intermediate bond fund to get steady growth as time goes by. "There's only been one year since the Depression in which bonds have lost money. So, you look at the bond market as a place where you're going to have assured growth," he says.

For people who can't afford the money necessary to ladder Treasury bonds, Self recommends investing in an intermediate bond fund, like the Rembrandt Fixed Income Fund, which he manages at ABN AMRO. These types of funds also own corporate bonds and mortgages. "You get a little more yield before fees from that kind of fund, because corporates and mortgages have more yield than the Treasuries of the same maturity. They have to yield more in order to get people to deviate from the safeness of Treasury securities," he says. "Your hope is that you are going to earn more than the 6% you can get from buying Treasury securities, because you're taking more risk by owning corporate and mortgage securities."

Unlike the stock market, investing in bonds doesn't require that you monitor their performance. Self says to forget the bonds until they mature. "You shouldn't be trading Treasuries, because the commissions are relatively high. They will go up and down in price with interest rates. But if you're holding them until maturity, you know

INTERMEDIATE BONDS

Intermediate bonds have up to 10 years of maturity. Self says any bond with a maturity longer than 10 years is not worth the risk. "What I usually recommend is a ladder approach to owning intermediate bonds. You own bonds every year from 2 years to 10 years, and as the bonds come due, you reinvest the proceeds in 10-year bonds. You're not trying to play the bond market or interest rates, you're just getting whatever yields are available at the time you're investing," he says.

The different types of intermediate bonds include corporates, mortgage-backed securities, tax-free bonds, and Treasuries. The intermediate bonds that Self recommends investing in are Treasury securities. "It's the easiest thing to do, because you buy them directly from the Federal Reserve auction. There are 2-, 3-, 5-, and 10-year Treasuries. You don't have to pay a commission, and there are no fees. You just have to contact the local Federal Reserve bank and get the information on participating in those auctions," he says. "You can buy them in the secondary market, but then you're going to pay a commission and the commissions tend to be relatively high. You're better off buying the Treasury securities at an auction."

To invest through the Federal Reserve, call the Federal Reserve bank in your region and request an application form. There are 12 regional branches across the United States (see Appendix C for listing). The application forms are called noncompetitive tenders, and the minimum is $1,000.

"They'll ask how much of par value bonds do you want, and you just write a check for that amount. You'll get whatever yield occurs in the auction, and then you'll get your coupon payments twice a year from the Treasury. The Treasury also has a program called the Treasury Direct Program, in which those coupons can go into an account, which you can reinvest in other Treasury securities. The return you get depends on the maturity," Self says.

He estimates that a two-year Treasury bond will yield about 5.85% and a 10-year bond about 6.15%. For the best effect, Self again mentions laddering the Treasury securities. "In the beginning what you might do is participate in the 2-, 3-, 5-, and 10-year auctions so that you'll have a bond coming due every year. Then you try to fill up the ladder so that you'll always have a bond coming due every year from 2 years out to 10 years. That's the ultimate goal," he says.

what you're going to get. So, it doesn't matter what happens in between times. It's only if you have to sell that you have to be concerned. But, if you're going to hold the bond—like you should—at the time that it matures you're going to get back the money you put in there, and you also will have gotten those interest payments over the years," he says. Simply put, bonds are a way to get income or steady growth.

For investors willing to take more risk, Self recommends investing in high-yield bond mutual funds (also known as junk bonds). Self says that in general 80% of your bond portfolio should be invested in Treasury bonds and 20% in high-yield bond funds in order to get more growth. You can invest in a high-yield bond mutual fund through a major mutual fund company. "They have tremendous volatility. In 1995, the returns were in the 20% to 30% range. But in 1989 or 1990, when people became concerned that the economy was going into a recession, the returns were negative 10% to 20%. It's a step in between owning bonds and owning stocks. Stocks are even riskier than high-yield bonds are, but you still can lose money in a high-yield bond fund. If you expect over time that intermediate-term bonds are going to earn 6% and stocks earn 10%, then high-yield bond funds will earn about 8%," he says.

Self added that people in the 31% tax bracket and higher should consider tax-exempt bonds, which are bonds issued by municipalities, authorities, and public entities. "I would go the mutual fund route because of the high commission costs, especially in the tax-exempt market. There are very high commissions attached to buying individual bonds, and unless you have a million or more you can't get proper diversification by owning individual tax-exempt bonds," he says. "It doesn't make sense to buy bonds longer than 10 years, though, because you don't get enough yield to lock it in for a longer period of time. But, you will need a broker or financial planner to help you purchase individual tax-exempt bonds. There's no direct program like there is on the Treasury side. You have to buy them on the open market."

With tax-exempt bond funds you get a lower yield, but the advantage is that you don't have to pay taxes on it. "Unless your tax bracket is high enough, it's not worthwhile to have the tax exemption because the yield you'll get is too low to compensate you for the tax exemption," he says.

The rule of thumb for asset allocation, Self says, is that your age should be the percentage you have invested in bonds. So, for example, if you are 43, 43% of your assets should be invested in bonds and the remaining 57% should be invested in stocks. "It's a very good rule, because it forces you, when you're young, to have a very high percentage in stocks. But even when you become 60 or 65, you shouldn't get out of the stock market altogether because you'll still probably live another 20 years," he says.

Self says it's equally important to diversify internationally on the equity side. "There's no reason to be xenophobic in this world in which we are all in it together. Any company that you work for is likely to be affected somewhat by what is going on internationally, and so one should have international exposure," he says.

With a $50,000 inheritance, Self says for a 40-year-old he would recommend $30,000 in stocks, $15,000 in a tax-exempt bond fund, and $5,000 in a high-yield bond fund. With $50 to invest on a monthly basis, Self says to invest it in an intermediate bond fund, or in a tax-exempt bond fund if your tax bracket is in the 31% range.

Watch out for long maturities and illiquidity. "The more yield you get on a security, the more risk you're taking. The longer it is to maturity, the more risk you're taking that inflation will eat away at your principal value. The intermediate bond is not too long, whereas with 30-year bonds a lot could happen 30 years from now that none of us can foresee. The other thing you have to be careful of is liquidity. If you have to sell, you'll pay a high commission. So you don't want all of your portfolio in illiquid bonds. But, when you're in a mutual fund, then you have tremendous liquidity because if you need to sell, you get your money back at the value of the bonds that day. You don't pay a commission," he says.

THE LAST WORD

"THE SECRET IS TO SAVE REGULARLY AND BE DIVERsified. We always save at least 10% of our income each pay period and the power of compound interest ends up working for us. Having an investment that works out well—such as strips—helps, also. The other secret of getting what I've gotten is by concentrating on my career and working hard to be able to be compensated quite well so that I have more to save," Self says.

Chapter 18

Maceo Sloan is chairman, president, and CEO of Sloan Financial Group, Inc. He received his B.A. from Morehouse College and M.B.A. from Georgia State University. He currently resides in Bahama, North Carolina, with his wife and two children.

MACEO SLOAN

GENERALLY SPEAKING, MACEO SLOAN IS A PULL-yourself-up-by-the-bootstraps kind of man.

His story begins back in 1898 when Sloan's ancestors started up the North Carolina Mutual Life Insurance Company, the nation's largest black-owned life insurance company, headquartered in Durham, North Carolina. Sloan was fourth-generation management, spending a total of 13 years with the family-owned business. His last position was vice president, treasurer, and chief investment officer.

In 1974, Sloan made a proposal to his family's insurance company to start a money management firm. Finally, in November 1986, NCM Capital Management Group, an investment money management firm, was born. It was the first black-owned money management firm based in North Carolina and the fifth in the United States. "We manage for most of the major municipalities in the country, for a dozen different states, and for a number of Fortune 500 companies. We also manage money for colleges, universities, and foundations," he says.

NCM Capital was started to diversify the insurance company. It was a financial services company with an insurance base. But in 1991, North Carolina Mutual returned to operating solely as an insurance company. "We formed the Sloan Financial Group as a holding company to buy 100% ownership interest of NCM Capital from the insurance company. As a result, NCM Capital is no longer affiliated with the insurance company. We sold 40% of the Sloan Financial Group to IDS Capital Holdings, which is a subsidiary of American Express. Together, we paid several million for NCM Capital. We formed the holding company to get the rest of the money we needed to buy NCM Capital from the life insurance company," Sloan explains.

Sloan owns 60% of the Sloan Financial Group along with his protégé Justin Beckett. Sloan is chairman, president, and CEO of the Sloan Financial Group. The Sloan Financial Group in turn owns 100% of NCM Capital and 100% of New Africa Advisers, an international money management operation that was started in 1993. Both NCM Capital and New Africa Advisers manage mutual funds. The only difference is that NCM Capital manages funds for the Dreyfus Corporation and for the Calvert Group while New Africa Advisers manages funds for Calvert Sloan Advisors, which is an affiliate of the Calvert Group, a white-owned fund family.

Calvert Sloan Advisors is another aspect of Sloan's business, split 50–50 between the Calvert Group and Sloan Holdings. Started in 1995, Calvert Sloan Advisors is a subsidiary of Sloan Holdings, another of Sloan's three holding companies. The other holding company is Sloan Communications, which is a controlling shareholder of Conxus, formerly known as PCS Development, a technology company that is building a nationwide advance paging system.

Why so many holding companies? Sloan says it's for tax purposes. "Some of these companies we'll take public and some we will not. When you have a collection of companies they are all treated differently taxwise, so you can't throw them all in one pot. That doesn't work. Part of it is also estate planning," he says.

Together, NCM Capital and New Africa Advisers are now managing about $4 billion. When you are in charge of that kind of money, you must have some ideas on what people can be doing with their money. Sloan says first and foremost African-Americans need to concentrate on the generation of wealth rather than on spending it.

"We make a lot of money but we spend every dime we

get. There's very little in terms of investment that we do as a people. We consume our income rather than invest it, and therefore there's little passed on to the next generation. Typically, when you look at the black family, the parents die and children are happy to have money left over to bury them with, but no legacy is passed on to jump-start the next generation," Sloan says. "The first thing we can do is invest our money instead of spending. Set aside a minimum of 15% of your income for investing (and your investments need to run the gamut, from mutual funds to real estate holdings), and look to some venture capital limited partnership holdings."

Sloan recommends approaching black broker-dealers about limited partnership opportunities. He says the average annual return is 30% over a five- to seven-year period. "If we were thinking right, we'd go to the black broker-dealers and say 'I have an interest in this type of investment,' because if you go to the white broker-dealers, the deals are going to be with majority companies. You won't see any minority companies trying to raise money in this manner," Sloan says. "If you go to the black broker-dealers, they are going to know about minority companies offering this opportunity. We need to invest money back into our own communities, and limited partnerships is one way to do that."

The minimum investment can be as low as $2,000 for IRAs and as high as $100,000. Sloan offered a limited partnership to raise part of the money for PCS Development. The minimum was $100,000. He says not having that kind of money to invest in limited partnerships is an excuse. PCS, now known as Conxus, has 80 limited partners, all of whom are minorities, including women.

"We make nice money in this country. We go to the

VENTURE CAPITAL LIMITED PARTNERSHIP HOLDING INVESTMENTS

A partnership is one type of business organization. Other business organizations include sole proprietorship and incorporation. A limited partnership has one general partner and many limited partners. The general partner sells units to investors, who become limited partners. The general partner holds all responsibility for the operations of the partnership, such as investing the capital raised, managing the partnership's business, and performing the necessary accounting procedures. In the prospectus, you will find the financial terms, sales charges, expenses, conflicts of interest, investment objectives, and risk considerations. There are two types of limited partnerships. They include direct participation programs (DPPs) and master limited partnerships (MLPs).

DPPs are "private" limited partnerships where the units do not normally have a liquid secondary market. They are designed to be held long-term, 10 to 15 years or longer.

MLPs are "public" limited partnerships where the units have a secondary market and normally will trade on the NYSE, AMEX, or NASDAQ. They are usually formed in two ways: (1) by combining several DPPs that have the same general partner and the same business operation, and (2) by distributing a portion of a corporation's assets to form an MLP.

Source: The Investing Kit by Bay Gruber, © 1996 by Dearborn Financial Publishing, Inc. Published by Dearborn Financial Publishing, Inc. All rights reserved. Reprinted with permission.

Sloan says limited partnerships are often where new companies get second-stage financing to expand their business. "They'll form a limited partnership and will raise money from different people by having them buy limited partner shares. You have no further liability when you purchase limited partnership interest," he says. "Basically, you're pooling your money, and the group typically invests in new companies that are seeking second-stage financing."

same schools that white people go to. We have significant opportunities. I see black people driving BMWs and Mercedeses. If we'd stop buying fancy clothes and cars, we'd have money to put into these types of investments. We need to adjust our priorities," he says. "Black America has been raised to be a nation of consumers, which is why we don't control a significant amount of assets in America, and we need to change that."

Sloan practices what he preaches, living below his means. For example, Sloan says he chooses to drive a Jeep, when in fact he could be driving a Rolls-Royce. "I live on the amount I need to live on and invest the rest. I spend a reasonable amount of money doing things. I don't spend money just because I have it. When I do spend money, it's for an investment, such as art or investment-grade jewelry. It's the quality that counts rather than type. I also take little money out of my companies, because I can grow it faster by leaving it in the company. I only take out the amount that I need. In terms of my salary and bonus, I don't take out as much as I could," he says.

PERSONAL PORTFOLIO

Although Sloan would not disclose the contents of his personal portfolio or give any stock recommendations (he says he doesn't want to mislead readers into making a faulty investment), he did reveal what mutual funds he's invested in. They include the Dreyfus Third Century Fund, the Calvert New Africa Fund, and the Calvert Managed Growth Fund. In terms of picking stocks for his clients Sloan was a little more forthcoming.

"We look for companies that are undervalued and that

have a growing earnings trend, for companies that surprise the Street in terms of earnings. We look at companies that make a little bit more money every quarter. We take the four quarters and compare them to the previous four quarters, moving back one quarter. It's called earnings momentum," he says. "We also look at fundamentals to make sure the company is sound. We ask questions such as how good is management, how consistent is management, how reactive is the company to changes in the marketplace, how dominant are they in their industry, are they staying current with the trends in the industry, are they doing things in the best interest of the shareholder, and are they good corporate citizens. For that, we examine employment practices, the way they treat their employees and the environment. We consider whether they are active in the communities."

When asked about his single most important investment, Sloan says it is certainly his education. Sloan has a B.A. in business administration and economics from Morehouse College, an MBA from Georgia State University, and a J.D. from North Carolina Central University School of Law, the largest black school in the state.

"My education is what enables me to do all the things I can do. You have to have the proper training to understand how to do these things. It's not luck," he says, expounding upon his philosophy. "Luck is when opportunity meets preparation. If you take the time to prepare yourself, when the opportunity comes along you can take advantage of it. If you're not prepared, people say it's bad luck—and luck has little to do with it. I've never met anyone who has not had at least one opportunity come along in their lifetime."

Sloan says he's worth well over $10 million. His secret to amassing such a large personal fortune is that he's been a risk taker. The biggest risk he's ever taken was when he started NCM Capital. At the time he resigned from the insurance company, he was very comfortable. He taught as an adjunct professor at a local law school. He was also of counsel to Moore and Van Allen, the largest law firm in North Carolina. "I was making good money when I resigned. Since NCM Capital was a subsidiary of the insurance company, I had a salary; but it was less than what I was making before. Looking back, the risk was worth it," he says.

His second biggest risk was forming Sloan Financial Group in order to buy NCM Capital from the insurance company. He took out a multimillion-dollar loan to do it, and today he's reaping the benefits of these risks. "When we bought NCM Capital we had about $500 million under management, which was six years ago. Today we have $4 billion under management," he says.

Still, in spite of his business success, Sloan says he still can't get a loan from mainstream banks today, and that this is indicative of how difficult it is to run a business as an African-American in this country.

"You can't borrow any significant money. You have to be very creative when you start asking for real money—they won't give it to you. They'll loan you money to buy a car or house. But to borrow large sums of money, it's just not available. Whereas with whites the bank looks at family, business history, and what they have accomplished and the decision is based on background and character and numbers, with blacks, it's based solely on numbers. Banks don't care about background and character with blacks. In order to get the money, you have to show that you don't need it, which is a Catch-22," he says. "There's no real source for capital to expand or build a business for African-Americans in this country, and once you get the business past a certain point, the black financial institutions are too small to help."

This is why African-Americans need to become innovative in the way that they generate wealth. One way to do that is by investing more aggressively. Sloan believes that African-Americans are too conservative with the investment money they do manage to save.

INVESTING ADVICE: STICK TO STOCK MUTUAL FUNDS

"We have a tendency to put money in CDs, which is the worst place to put it. We should be invested in the stock market. If you take any 10-year period, the stock market has outperformed the bond and CD market. And over the last 50 years, the market has averaged a 10%-a-year return. The bond market has been little better than half of that," he says.

In fact, Sloan recommends that individuals avoid having a portfolio of stocks. "I would suggest that African-Americans put their money in stock mutual funds because they don't have the time to pick stocks," he says. But if someone happens to have a stock portfolio, Sloan advises having at least 12 to 15 stocks in the portfolio, spread over a number of sectors in the marketplace.

The perfect asset allocation for a 30-year-old single individual, according to Sloan, is 100% in stock mutual funds. About 25% should be in small-cap mutual fund names, 10% to 15% in international funds—including emerging markets, Europe, Asia, Latin America, and Africa—and the rest should be in mid-to-large-cap funds. First, though, Sloan recommends having six months of salary saved up in a liquid asset. You should also have some type of life insurance in place, such as term insurance.

With a hypothetical $50,000 inheritance, Sloan says to put it in a mutual fund and just leave it, assuming that you don't need it for other purposes.

THE LAST WORD

"**B**LACKS NEED TO GO TO BLACK BROKERAGE FIRMS, because we need to start doing business with each other and see if we can't help each other instead of shunning each other. If we don't, there's not going to be any African-American financial future. If we pour money into other communities and not into the black community, we will be second-class citizens forever," he says.

Part VI

TRADING

Chapter 19

Harold Doley, Jr., is chairman of Doley Securities. He received his B.S. from Xavier University in Louisiana and O.P.M. from Harvard University. He currently resides in Irvington, New York, with his wife and two children.

HAROLD DOLEY, JR.

A S ONE OF THE MORE PROMINENT AFRICAN-AMERI-
cans on Wall Street, Harold Doley, Jr., owns his securities firm and a seat on the New York Stock Exchange,
and is a member of Lloyd's of London, among other things.

I'd originally met Doley at a National Association of
Black Journalists convention in Philadelphia in August
1995. At the time, I was working as the personal finance
editor at *Black Enterprise* magazine and naturally wanted
to talk to this mover and shaker. The Doleys live in
Madame C. J. Walker's 30-room mansion. Walker was
America's first black millionairess at the turn of the century. Today, the estate is a National Historical Landmark.

"My most important investment is Madame C. J.
Walker's mansion, because it's wonderful to live in this
old historic home with so much African-American history.
And, the interest on my mortgage is a tax deduction," he
said. "I buy a lot of art and for years it was housed at a mu-
seum in New Orleans. When I bought the mansion, I
brought all of my art to the house."

During our interview, Doley was poised, calm, and
collected, and he didn't mince any words in sharing his secrets. He secured his successes by using whatever program
or perk available.

The key to financial success, according to Doley, is to
set goals and have one mind-set in meeting those goals. In
addition, he believes that you have to invest in yourself
through education and thinking positively. Finally, he says
it's critical to have a mate or spouse who understands your
goals. Doley has followed these three strategies and is
reaping the rewards.

The 50-year-old has come a long way from his hum-
ble beginnings in New Orleans, Louisiana. He was named
one of the wealthiest African-Americans in 1996 by *Se-*

curities Pro Newsletter with an estimated worth of $25 million.

He was the first African-American individual to buy a seat on the New York Stock Exchange, in 1973, five years after graduating from Xavier University. He was 26 years old. Owning real estate provided him with the foundation he needed to purchase the seat. "The first thing you should do is invest in a house," he says. "Save and put money aside to buy a house."

When he was 20 years old, Doley bought a double house in New Orleans for $22,000 at a government auction. Each side had three bedrooms, two full baths, living room, dining room, foyer, and utility room, with front and back yards. He rented one side of the house for $300 a month, which paid his mortgage. He lived rent-free in the other side.

"I went and borrowed the money from a savings and loan, which was an African-American savings and loan. I was young and had no credit, but I did have an account at the savings and loan. It was United Federal Savings and Loan," Doley says in his slight Southern drawl. "But the house was in bad shape. I had to renovate it, and I was able to get the money to do that from the savings and loan." Doley believes so much in this real estate strategy that he mentioned it in a speech he gave at Harvard Business School in 1972. If he were 20 years younger, Doley says, today he'd buy up inner-city property.

"The name of the speech was 'From Skin Popping to Mainlining.' It was a street thing. I talked about how to develop a mom-and-pop business in the ghetto and making it into a publicly held company. My formula was go and save and have shelter that pays your mortgage by owning your own home and benefiting from rental income," he says.

TIPS FOR FIRST-TIME HOME BUYERS

- There are a few programs geared for first-time buyers. You can get a mortgage from your state or local housing agency. When you call, say that you are a first-time home buyer looking for a mortgage. To find the local or state housing agency, look in the yellow pages of your phone book under "housing authority."
- There are "Fannie Mae" or "Freddie Mac" loans for first-time home buyers. "Fannie Mae" is the Federal National Mortgage Association (800-832-2345) and "Freddie Mac" is the Federal Home Loan Mortgage Corporation (800-FREDDIE). Call 800-688-HOME for a copy of Fannie's publication "Opening the Door to a Home of Your Own."
- You can also get help through the Federal Housing Authority. Contact your local Housing and Urban Development (HUD) office. If you've been in the armed services, the Department of Veteran Affairs offers some help. Call 800-827-1000 for information.

Doley has relied heavily on black banks to help him achieve his goal; he would advise everyone to befriend an African-American banker.

"There have been times in my life when a majority financial institution would tell me no and a black institution would tell me yes because I knew the people at the African-American institution," he says. "Go to your nearest black bank and set up an appointment with the loan officer, or hopefully you'll know someone within the bank who can make an introduction for you."

According to Doley, when it comes to banks, there are

BLACK BANKERS

There are some organizations that will help you contact black bankers in your area. Try calling the Urban Bankers Coalition at 212-493-4388. You can also call the National Association of Federal Credit Unions and ask for a list of black-owned credit unions (800-336-4644). Creative Investment Research, based in Washington, DC, provides information and research on minority- and women-owned banks and thrifts. Call them at 202-722-5000 or check out their Web site at http://www2.ari.net/cirm.

---

three things to keep in mind: character, credit, and collateral. Doley says it pays to know your banker if you have bad credit, because then you can rely on character. And, if you own your own home, you can use it as collateral. "Pristine credit in the black community is virtually nonexistent. We have little credit and poor credit records so you have to weigh those three Cs. If you have good character and the bank knows who you are, they'll rely on character instead of credit. That's why it's important to befriend a banker."

African-American banks played a big part in Doley's rise to the top. His seat on the New York Stock Exchange cost him $90,000. He used his real estate as collateral, approaching a small black bank, the Small Business Administration (SBA), and a majority bank. He put together a package where the SBA would pay if he defaulted. "That was how I gathered $90,000 along with the other collateral I had from investments, stocks, bonds, savings, and refinanced property," he says. Doley sees the seat as an intangible asset that will always have value despite the naysayers who thought his investment was a bad one back in the mid-1970s. His return on the seat every year—about $180,000—is twice what he paid for it. If someone were to buy a seat on the exchange today, it would cost about $1.5 million.

Doley had set the goal of owning a seat on the New York Stock Exchange long ago when he was just a kid. He saw it as a way to make money; his motto—there's always money to be made where money is exchanged. "It's truly the meeting place of buyers and sellers," he says. He's owned the seat for 24 years now and leases it to a group with whom he has a partnership.

Doley first visited the New York Stock Exchange when he was 11 years old while on a family vacation. Doley was buying and selling stocks at 13 years old. Some of his first investments included Fuji Photo, Power Designs, ADP, and Toth Aluminum. "I wasn't playing the nifty fifty. I was going for big growth, and volume. I'd always wanted to be in business for myself and I wanted to be an investor," he says. "I was very young and I would take chances. You know you leverage yourself much more when you're young because the older you get the more you have to conserve. I was playing the stock and bond market and leveraging to the max."

After graduating from Xavier, Doley went to work for Prudential Securities (then known as Bache), where he trained to become a broker. He secured accounts nobody else seemed to want: black insurance companies, black colleges, black churches, and black banks.

In 1984, Doley became a member of Lloyd's of London, a 300-year-old insurance market. It cost him $600,000. To come up with the money, he pledged assets to Lloyd's with letters of credit from banks. The assets he pledged were stocks and bonds.

Lloyd's is made up of some of the richest people in the world, and there are very few black names. Members participate in syndicates that buy and sell insurance risk. "You receive premiums and then you have to pay out claims," Doley says. "I was recommended by another member, and I have a lot of money tied up in Lloyd's."

From 1988 to 1992, Lloyd's lost a total of $12.8 billion. But Doley was lucky—he had stepped out just in time. "I didn't underwrite for four years because I didn't like the profit margins that were available. I waited to return to the Lloyd's market in 1993, which brings me to the most important aspect of investing, which is: It's not where you buy an asset but where you sell it," he says. "You have to know when to get out, and that's the hardest part of investing. It's not wise to get married to stock and real estate investments."

Doley learned that lesson from his father, who owned a neighborhood grocery store. He says that when a major food chain set up shop five blocks away, his father knew that it was time to get out of the grocery business As a result, Doley's father went back to school to get his teaching certificate.

PERSONAL PORTFOLIO

Doley admits that when it comes to investing he's more of a trader than a long-term investor, but even the pros make mistakes. "I can remember when I sold too early or when I could have gotten more in negotiations. But hopefully those mistakes make me better in the long term. You're going to make mistakes, if you're out there swinging," he says.

His only long-term strategy applies to his nonfinancial assets, including real estate, the NYSE seat, the Lloyd's of London membership (members are referred to as names), and his firm, Doley Securities. His NYSE seat and his real estate assets made it easier for Doley to secure the $25,000 he needed to open his business in 1975. He approached the Minority Enterprise Small Business Investment Company, a privately owned venture capitalist firm. The firm, which receives subsidized money from the SBA at a lower rate, required that he take out a second mortgage on some of his real estate. "You have to use leverage, and the only way to use it is to have something to borrow against, which goes back to owning a home," he says. Doley Securities employs 22 clerks and 11 floor brokers. It is a joint venture with a partnership of other brokers who are members of the exchange. Doley is the only black in the group.

These days, Doley says he's trading in and out of Microsoft, Intel, Haliburton (an oil service company), and Disney. He recommends investing in oil and gas companies, which have given him growth and have appreciated in value. Some oil and gas companies Doley recommends include Baker Hughes and Texaco.

He promises to become more active in the emerging African markets because he sees a future for himself there. Doley, a Republican, was appointed by former President Ronald Reagan as the American ambassador and executive director of the African Development Bank in Abidjan, which finances projects for African railroads, schools, and hospitals. He served from 1983 to 1985.

Some African investments in his personal portfolio include Ashanti Gold, a Ghanaian gold company, and Consolidated Mining of South Africa, a gold and diamond mining company. "Generally, I buy what others don't want for a long-term investment, but I participate in the trend on a short-term basis. If the trend is up, you go with it on a short-term basis. But long-term, you buy when everybody else is selling," he says. "My true fortune will be made in Africa, and I'll be making a greater contribution."

He wakes up at 4:30 A.M. every weekday morning to check the overseas market, in particular Japan, Johannesburg, and London. But despite his assets and net worth, Doley doesn't consider himself a big player.

INVESTING ADVICE: BE A RISK-TAKER

Doley is conservative when it comes to his own money. He puts 40% of his income after taxes into savings. But young investors should be more risk-oriented, he says. His rule is that if you're in your twenties or thirties, invest up to 75% in stocks. "There will be times when you make a 25% return and other times when you'll make only 3% or 4% a year," he says. "On a short-term basis you want to participate in the trend. For the long term, go against the trend. If investors are selling something and it's worthless, buy it and hold it. Basically, you want what others don't want, like investing in inner-city property."

But, Doley cautions against investing in something without fully understanding it or when you don't feel at ease with it. Doley says you have to believe wholeheartedly in your investment. "If you don't believe in it, don't own it. You have to use all of the analysis that you can and then apply common sense to your investment decision," he says.

Regardless of the amount of money you make, invest whatever amount you can afford, whether it is $10, $100, or $1,000. Doley says it's important you have an investment plan and stick to the plan to provide for your child's college education, your retirement, or a second home. "Invest as much as you can after maintaining your standard of living. You must have a plan and set aside a certain amount every payday just like you put aside money for your mortgage or car note," he says.

THE LAST WORD

IF THERE'S ONE MESSAGE DOLEY HAS FOR AFRICAN-Americans, it's that all rewards are not financial. "African-Americans should look for rewards in family. Most of us, when we invest, invest for the security. So that's what really comes first and provides peace of mind," he says. "Investing can afford you a different lifestyle, a more secure life, and many of the things that you need to make life better for yourself and your family."

Chapter 20

HERB HARRIS

Herb Harris is executive vice president of Dimon Oil Corporation. He received his B.A. from Pace University. He currently lives in Queens, New York, with his wife and son.

HERB HARRIS IS ONE OF THREE BLACK OIL TRADERS on Wall Street. He and a partner founded Dimon Oil Corporation in 1987.

It's been a long haul to his current position of executive vice president of Dimon. He started on Wall Street with the Hartford Trust Company as a clerk after graduating from college in 1973. In 1976, he took a job with White Weld & Company, a brokerage house, which was taken over by Merrill Lynch. He worked as an accountant for Merrill Lynch until 1978. That's when Harris made a discovery.

"I walked on the trading floor, heard all the excitement, all the yelling and screaming, and wanted to know what it was. My friend explained that it was commodity trading and the gold market. What really got me was that if the price of gold went from $186.10 to $186.20, you were making $5 every time it ticked one point. That's $50. I said, 'I want to learn more about this business,' and I was hooked. I put in for a transfer to the commodities department right away. It was a calling even though I couldn't understand a word they were saying," he says. "My transfer came through two weeks later, and I became a runner to learn the basics. I had to start off as the low man on the totem pole, and I worked my way up from runner to Teletype™ clerk to phone clerk. Then, I became a market watcher and a market analyst. Then, I ran my own department."

By about 1987, Harris grew restless. He saw opportunity in the oil futures market and wanted to start his own company, but he didn't have the money to do it. He left Merrill Lynch for Mercoil Company, where he got a better base salary and received commissions on all of the money he was generating. About a year and a half later he found the partner he was looking for.

"I was looking to do something different in terms of trading activities on the floor. I looked around for a partner because I didn't have money to go on my own. It wasn't until I took a job at Mercoil Company in 1987 that I found someone to go into business with. I laid the groundwork in terms of clients and then found someone in that company who was willing to strike out on their own with me," he says. "The only capital we needed at the time was just a seat on the exchange, which was readily available because my partner had one. But we didn't have the capital to get more than one membership available to us. We got our clients from people on the Street we knew from past relationships who were working for themselves as commodity trading advisers (CTAs) trading oil."

Start-up costs included money for trading for the first month, which was about $7,000 or $8,000 in capital, he says. "It was fairly inexpensive, because what we really needed was a booth to work out of and telephones, obviously. As more customers came on board we had a decent level of success in terms of executing trades. That's the most important factor—being able to execute trades for customers and having them trust you," he says. "When you get into brokerage execution, cost is not that much, especially when you start off small. It's not very difficult to turn a profit in the first few months. If you start off big, then it gets expensive because you need telephone space and staff. In this business, big is anything over three people."

Harris stays in the trading booth with the telephone while his partner is in the trading ring. It's a 60–40 relationship with Harris getting only 40% of the company's profits. "Since the membership is in my partner's name, he has more risk. We make decisions together, but in terms of splitting profits, he gets a higher percentage of the profits," he says.

In its first month, Dimon Oil, which has since added three new employees, generated about $12,000 in revenues, according to Harris. Today, eight years later, the company is generating about $1 million a year in revenues.

Harris was reluctant to pinpoint his net worth, saying only that it is over $100,000 but less than $500,000. He says not being able to put his profits back into the futures market helped him amass his personal fortune. "I took my profits and put them in more stable investment vehicles, such as stocks. I never did like the mutual funds or commodity funds. I have no real interest in any of these," he says.

INVESTING ADVICE: TAKE RISKS AND LOOK
BEYOND STOCKS AND MUTUAL FUNDS

Despite being a conservative investor, Harris's general advice to the African-American public is look at investment alternatives aside from the usual stocks and mutual funds. "The alternative does come with risk but it can be managed. You want to look at all the potential that's out there. Don't be locked into the paper stuff on TV in terms of bonds, Treasury bills, stocks, and mutual funds. Become more entrepreneurial and more willing to take risks. Get out of the comfort zone, which is what I did to start the company. It was a big risk because I had a family and debts," he says. "If you have $50,000 or $60,000, be willing to take the risk and manage the risk properly to go out on your own and create an income for yourself, whether it be primary or secondary. We need to see more blacks doing this in the business."

In terms of investment vehicles, Harris says African-Americans should consider investing in futures, even though that area is highly risky. "It doesn't necessarily have to be oil. There's the futures market and the derivatives market. It's all available, but we as African-Americans don't find the time or the money to put in there. Most of it has to do with the fact that we're not up to date about what's available in the financial world. I'd look into the agricultural end of it, and financial futures such as T-bond futures, T-note futures, Treasury bill futures, and currency futures. They sound sophisticated, but they're fairly simple. You just have to learn the concept behind it," he says.

In general, the concept behind the futures market, Harris says, involves taking risks that within minutes can produce returns on your money that are not normally done over such a short period of time. "You're betting on future productivity, future demand, and future world problems. You're anticipating what hot spots are going to flare up and how they are going to affect price movements of any given commodity, futures, or currency transaction," he says.

Harris applies his knowledge of the futures market to the stock market. The investment he's still reaping benefits from is a $5,000 investment in stocks five years ago that is now worth well over $20,000. "I try to keep away from what I trade, so I don't invest in oil futures. I invest in the stocks of oil companies, in companies that are futures-related, such as orange juice companies. I trade in and out of Tropicana because the colder the winter, the higher the price. I don't invest in it if the price is high. You want to look at orange juice in the off-season; that's when you want to buy it. The same thing goes for coffee. I just sold my shares in Chock Full o' Nuts and Starbucks because the price of coffee went up," he says.

Right now, Harris is high on oil exploration and drilling companies. He's holding Mobil stock and just bought shares in Ethyl, an oil refinery, because he reasons that there will be a long-term demand for plastic items in the future, and plastics are oil-based. Harris advises looking into companies that offer alternatives to oil, such as natural gas companies. He's currently holding stock in Tesoro Petroleum and Elf-Acquataine, two natural gas companies.

Although he's not a stock picker, Harris has had good luck with some of the stocks he's bought. For example, he bought shares in Freeport McMoran, an oil services company that provides towboat services to offshore oil rigs, at

$9 and got out at $24. He bought stock in Tesoro Petro-leum for $4.50 a share and sold it at $15. He bought it again at $9 and now it's hovering at $12. "I'll see if it goes up any higher, because I really think natural gas is going to be the way to go. Tesoro is transforming themselves from being a crude oil–related corporation to being a natural gas corporation," he says.

Pressed for more information on why he doesn't in-vest in the futures market, Harris says, "The Commodi-ties Futures Trading Commission (CFTC) rules say that I can't invest in futures positions as one who is advising or executing trades for customers within the commodity market. The second reason is just for my own sanity. I don't want to sit there all the time and keep track of my own commodities and I don't want to mix commodities and stocks together, because they are two different ani-mals. It's either-or," he says.

Harris says that investing in the futures market is good if you want a quick fix, but he stresses that it is risky. It may earn you a whole lot more than 10% to 12% a year in returns. "You can make 300% to 400%, but you need a minimum of $50,000—and you have to be willing to lose that $50,000. Some futures markets do chew up less of your money because the margin rates are lower, and some futures markets are way higher. The crude oil futures market is least expensive because you only need to put about $1,500 per contract to start creat-ing some sort of an income. Keep in mind that it's a fluid market, unlike the stock market. The $1,500 you're us-ing to leverage a contract today won't necessarily be there at the end of the day. You might lose it. With the stock market, if you put in $1,500, you might lose a dol-lar or two a day but you still have $1,400 available tomorrow. With crude oil, losing a dollar today means your $1,500 is gone. It's basically all or nothing," he says. "If someone says you only need $1,500 to invest in futures, he's probably a shyster. Any reputable brokerage house or commodity broker will ask for at least $50,000; that's the minimum."

Harris has some advice for those bold enough to want to try investing in the futures market. First, he says, research the commodity, whether it's gold, silver, oil, milk, sugar, coffee, or cocoa. "Know what makes the markets move, know the political ramifications, and know what impact the weather is going to have on the commodity. I can say more about oil because that's what I trade. So, I would say, for oil, know what the production levels are and what the demand is. Know what the political climate is at any given moment. You need to constantly keep on top of the news, because the picture can change from morning to afternoon. You need to know who the players are. In the oil market, keep track of Phibro, J. P. Morgan, the commodity fund players, and George Soros," he says.

The pitfalls of investing in the futures market include watching out for schemes. "There are people out there who will tell you, 'Give me X amount of dollars, I'll invest it for you and give you X return on your money.' Then, you never hear back from that person again after you give them your money. If you can't keep in contact with the person on a weekly basis, don't get involved. If you are told to invest in an overseas market, don't get involved, because there aren't too many overseas futures markets. Be wary if you're told about an oil well, or to invest in gasoline stations. Beware of cold calls or prospectuses in the mail," he says.

Harris doesn't recommend investing a $50,000 inheritance in the futures market. Instead, he suggests an asset allocation of 10% in cash, 30% in fixed income securities yielding a minimum of 9% to 10%, another 10% or $5,000 in some sort of direct marketing or franchise business, 10% to charity, 25% in a home or real estate property, and 15% in safe blue-chip stocks. "Young black kids, I notice, spend a lot of money on fashion. They might live in the poorest of homes or neighborhoods, but they will wear the most expensive clothes. What they need to do is become entrepreneurial and find a business to get into that will create a long-term residual income. They most certainly need to get into business for themselves," he says.

Instead of spending $50 on the latest fashion item, Harris recommends investing in dividend reinvestment plans (DRIPs). "I'd find a stock that's an established stock in the United States, like a utility stock, which has a high yield. Most utility stocks yield between 8.5% and 14%. Do the initial purchase of, say, $50 or $100, and every month do a dividend reinvestment in addition to purchasing more stock. Utilities are excellent investments. They don't move pricewise as quickly as some of your conventional stocks, but you can't beat the return on your money. For steady income-producing stocks, that's where I'd start," he says.

Harris's savings plan is wrapped up in his company's profit sharing plan. Per quarter, he stores anywhere from $2,000 to $3,000—that is his long-term savings plan. He says that he finds putting money in the bank costs him more than what it's worth because banks give only 3% interest while profit sharing provides 9% interest.

FIRMS THAT OFFER INITIAL PURCHASE ONLY FOR THEIR UTILITY CUSTOMERS

American Water Works ($100) 609-346-8200

Boston Edison ($500) 800-736-3001

Carolina Power & Light ($20) 919-546-6111

Cascade Natural Gas (WA, OR, $250) 206-624-3900

Central Hudson Gas & Electric (NY, $100) 914-452-2000 (offers to noncustomers)

Connecticut Energy ($250) 203-382-8156

Connecticut Water Service ($100) 203-669-8636

Dominion Resources (VA, $200) 800-552-4034 (offers to everybody)

Enova ($25) 619-696-2020 (offers to everybody)

Idaho Power ($10) 800-635-5406

IES Industries ($50) 800-247-9785

IWC Resources ($100) 317-639-1501

Keyspan Energy ($250) 718-403-3334

Minnesota Power & Light ($10) 218-723-3974 (offers to everybody)

National Fuel Gas (NY, PA, $200) 212-541-7533

Nevada Power ($25) 800-344-9239

New Jersey Resources ($25) 908-938-1230

Northwestern Public Service (SD, NE, $10) 605-352-8411

Philadelphia Suburban ($250) 215-527-8000 (offers to everybody)

Southwest Gas (NV, $100) 702-876-7280

Union Electric (MO, no minimum) 800-255-2237

United Water Resources (NY, NJ, $25) 201-767-2811

Source: According to Charles Carlson, author of *Buying Stocks without a Broker* (McGraw-Hill, 1996) and vice president of *DRIP Investor*, Hammond, IN (800-233-5922).

THE LAST WORD

"AMERICANS AS A WHOLE AREN'T GOOD SAVERS. I would say that we need to be saving. If your income bracket runs $40,000 to $50,000 a year, you need to be saving anywhere between 5% and 10%—preferably in a profit sharing plan, because with profit sharing you're allowed up to 13.5% in interest and that's a nice tidy sum to put away," Harris says.

APPENDIXES

Appendix A

BLACK-OWNED AND -MANAGED MUTUAL FUNDS

Profit Lomax Value Fund
Profit Lomax
8720 Georgia Avenue, Suite 808
Silver Spring, MD 20910
888-335-6629

Victory Lakefront Fund
Victory
1900 East Dublin-Granville Road
Columbus, OH 43229
800-539-3863

Ariel Growth
Ariel Appreciation Fund
Ariel Premier Bond Fund
307 North Michigan Avenue, Suite 500
Chicago, IL 60601-5305
800-725-0140

Calvert New Africa Fund
4550 Montgomery Avenue, Suite 1000-N
Bethesda, MD 20814-3343
800-368-2745

Lou Holland Growth Fund
Holland Capital Management
35 West Wacker Drive, Suite 3260
Chicago, IL 60601
800-522-2711

Kenwood Growth & Income
The Kenwood Group
10 South LaSalle Street, Suite 3610
Chicago, IL 60603
888-KEN-FUND

Brown Equity Fund
Brown Balanced Fund
Brown Small Company Fund
Brown Capital Management
809 Cathedral Street
Baltimore, MD 21201
800-809-FUND
800-525-FUND

Chapman Domestic Emerging Market Stocks Fund
Chapman U.S. Treasury Money Fund
Chapman Funds
World Trade Center
401 East Pratt Street, 28th Floor
Baltimore, MD 21202
800-752-1013

Appendix B

FEDERAL RESERVE SYSTEM LOCATIONS

Federal Reserve Bank of
Atlanta
104 Marietta Street, N.W.
Atlanta, GA 30303

Federal Reserve Bank of
Boston
600 Atlantic Avenue
Boston, MA 02106

Federal Reserve Bank of
Chicago
230 South La Salle Street
Chicago, IL 60690

Federal Reserve Bank of
Cleveland
1455 East 6th Street
Cleveland, OH 44101

Federal Reserve Bank of
Dallas
400 South Akard Street
Dallas, TX 75222

Federal Reserve Bank of
Kansas City
925 Grand Avenue
Kansas City, MO 64198

Federal Reserve Bank of
Minneapolis
250 Marquette Avenue
Minneapolis, MN 55480

Federal Reserve Bank of
New York
33 Liberty Street
New York, NY 10045

Federal Reserve Bank of
Philadelphia
Ten Independence Mall
Philadelphia, PA 19106

Federal Reserve Bank of
Richmond
701 East Byrd Street
Richmond, VA 23219

Federal Reserve Bank of
St. Louis
411 Locust Street
St. Louis, MO 63102

Federal Reserve Bank of
San Francisco
101 Market Street
San Francisco, CA 94105

Index

Financially fearless
by 40

Debt-free by
38
Jason Anthony